RESPECT

How to
Change the World
One Interaction
at a Time

RESPECT

ROBERT L. DILENSCHNEIDER

WILEY

Copyright © 2026 by John Wiley & Sons, Inc. All rights reserved, including rights for text and data mining and training of artificial intelligence technologies or similar technologies.

Published by John Wiley & Sons, Inc., Hoboken, New Jersey.
Published simultaneously in Canada.

No part of this publication may be reproduced, stored in a retrieval system, or transmitted in any form or by any means, electronic, mechanical, photocopying, recording, scanning, or otherwise, except as permitted under Section 107 or 108 of the 1976 United States Copyright Act, without either the prior written permission of the Publisher, or authorization through payment of the appropriate per-copy fee to the Copyright Clearance Center, Inc., 222 Rosewood Drive, Danvers, MA 01923, (978) 750-8400, fax (978) 750-4470, or on the web at www.copyright.com. Requests to the Publisher for permission should be addressed to the Permissions Department, John Wiley & Sons, Inc., 111 River Street, Hoboken, NJ 07030, (201) 748-6011, fax (201) 748-6008, or online at http://www.wiley.com/go/permission.

The manufacturer's authorized representative according to the EU General Product Safety Regulation is Wiley-VCH GmbH, Boschstr. 12, 69469 Weinheim, Germany, e-mail: Product_Safety@wiley.com.

Trademarks: Wiley and the Wiley logo are trademarks or registered trademarks of John Wiley & Sons, Inc. and/or its affiliates in the United States and other countries and may not be used without written permission. All other trademarks are the property of their respective owners. John Wiley & Sons, Inc. is not associated with any product or vendor mentioned in this book.

Limit of Liability/Disclaimer of Warranty: While the publisher and the authors have used their best efforts in preparing this work, including a review of the content of the work, neither the publisher nor the authors make any representations or warranties with respect to the accuracy or completeness of the contents of this work and specifically disclaim all warranties, including without limitation any implied warranties of merchantability or fitness for a particular purpose. No warranty may be created or extended by sales representatives, written sales materials or promotional statements for this work. The fact that an organization, website, or product is referred to in this work as a citation and/or potential source of further information does not mean that the publisher and authors endorse the information or services the organization, website, or product may provide or recommendations it may make. This work is sold with the understanding that the publisher is not engaged in rendering professional services. The advice and strategies contained herein may not be suitable for your situation. You should consult with a specialist where appropriate. Further, readers should be aware that websites listed in this work may have changed or disappeared between when this work was written and when it is read. Neither the publisher nor authors shall be liable for any loss of profit or any other commercial damages, including but not limited to special, incidental, consequential, or other damages.

For general information on our other products and services or for technical support, please contact our Customer Care Department within the United States at (800) 762-2974, outside the United States at (317) 572-3993 or fax (317) 572-4002.

Wiley also publishes its books in a variety of electronic formats. Some content that appears in print may not be available in electronic formats. For more information about Wiley products, visit our web site at www.wiley.com.

Library of Congress Cataloging-in-Publication Data is Available:

ISBN 9781394340965 (Cloth)
ISBN 9781394340972 (ePub)
ISBN 9781394340989 (ePDF)

Cover Design: Paul McCarthy
Cover Art: © Getty Images | Ali Kahfi

SKY10125589_090325

To Joan Avagliano, who is responsible for much of my success.

Books by Robert L. Dilenschneider

Character

The Ultimate Guide to Power & Influence

Nailing It

Decisions

The Critical First Years of Your Professional Life

50 Plus!

The Critical 2nd Phase of Your Professional Life

Power and Influence

Civility in America

The Public Relations Handbook

A Briefing for Leaders

The AMA Handbook of Public Relations

A Time for Heroes

Values for a New Generation

On Power

The Men of St. Charles

The Corporate Communications Bible

The Hero's Way

Contents

Preface		xi
Chapter 1	A Call for Respectfulness	1
Chapter 2	Is Respectfulness Truly Possible in the Age of Retribution?	19
Chapter 3	What's in It for Me?	37
Chapter 4	Start with Self-Respect	53
Chapter 5	The Top Five Qualities of Respectfulness	71
Chapter 6	Respectfulness at Work	89
Chapter 7	Respectfulness in Family and Personal Relationships	107
Chapter 8	Respectfulness in Civic Institutions	125
Chapter 9	Transforming Society	143
Notes		161
Acknowledgments		169
About the Author		171
Index		173

Preface

Respect may be one of the least discussed human qualities. Most of us go through life without giving it much thought. It seldom comes up in conversations. The media rarely use the word. It's not that we don't care about respect. Rather, we tend to just take it for granted.

It is my contention that respect deserves, well . . . more respect. That is, more attention, consideration, appreciation, praise.

It is respect for one another that builds healthy relationships. It is mutual respect that creates friendships and enables societies and their organizations to function effectively. It is respect that establishes trust between individuals, between groups, among nations.

It is the feeling of being respected that helps build self-confidence. And our own self-respect is essential for us to get along in life.

But if we don't think much about respect, we do give a lot of attention to its opposite: *disrespect*. We've even created a shorthand version of the word: *diss*. Just saying, "You dissed me" can be enough to start insults flying, and sometimes fists, too. Countless feuds have started because someone felt disrespected. In extreme cases, even wars.

To put it simply, being respectful for one another makes this a better world. Failing to show respect can make it a worse place. That's true not only in our daily lives but also throughout history. In fact, a lot of world history has been made by people who used respect as a force for good.

A carefully selected group of leaders and thinkers were interviewed for this book and their experiences and advice bring life to the lessons. They share their perspectives on how to embody and encourage respectfulness at work, with personal interactions of family and friends, and within the community.

I have long cared about the value of respectfulness; what I see as the erosion of it prompted this book.

I've encountered many, many people in my decades-long career in international public relations; I've been called the "dean of American public relations executives" and have written several books on the subject. Thirty-plus years ago I started my own Manhattan-based firm, The Dilenschneider Group, which provides strategic advice to Fortune 500 companies, leading families, and individuals around the world. Every day, business and political leaders come to me for advice. I will share with you real-world examples of what I've learned in my long career.

My curiosity about human nature compelled me to write books, such as *Decisions: Practical Advice from 23 Men and Women Who Shaped the World*, *Nailing It: How History's Awesome Twentysomethings Got It Together*, and more recently, *Character: Lessons in Courage, Integrity and Leadership*.

Concern about the eroding of civility in discourse prompted me to initiate a Civility in America lecture series, along with the Hearst Corporation. Many of the nation's thinkers from a wide variety of professions have been featured and provided a perspective on what must be done to restore civility. The series began in 2012 and, sad to say, civility is needed now more than ever.

Civility and respect go hand-in-hand.

My hope is that the exploration of respectfulness in this book will be helpful to you—whether you see the need or especially if you do not yet. The pages are packed with provocative thought and practical advice.

Here is your road map to restoring respectfulness in every facet of life and improving society along the way, one personal interaction at a time.

CHAPTER 1

A Call for Respectfulness

> *It's a gaze that radiates respect. It's a gaze that says that every person I meet is unique, unrepeatable, and, yes, superior to me in some way.*
>
> *Every person I meet is fascinating on some topic.*
>
> – David Brooks

The world can feel like it's fueled by chaos. Disorder is the new order. Our planet's 8.1 billion population is clamoring to be heard—all at once. Social media has handed the megaphone to any who want it, regardless of the truthfulness of what they have to say. And if the poster can remain anonymous, then it's no holds barred.

While instant communication comes with undeniable and remarkable benefits, the unfiltered platforms have encouraged nastiness and rancor as a means to get attention and gain followers. An innocuous comment, say about a beautiful sunrise, can quickly devolve into political diatribes and name-calling. Consensus building is supplanted by ostracizing "the other."

It seems that respect for each other is perceived as unnecessary, a virtue of a bygone era. Respect is like the pocket square tucked into a man's suit—an old-fashioned touch serving no purpose. Even suits are becoming optional for work these days!

Far from outdated, however, respectfulness is a vital part of the foundation of a well-functioning society and a fulfilling life. We would do well to cultivate it, and this book will show you how—and why.

Here is a good measure of just how important respect can be: one of the great shifts in the history of Western civilization came when it set aside a code of conduct based on honor and replaced it with a code based on, yes, respect. For centuries when one man said another had dishonored him, it all too often led to a duel. Now when an issue arises and one feels disrespected rather than dishonored, rancor may result, but no one gets run through with a sword or shot by a musket ball.

Yet that code of conduct is on shaky ground these days when respect for others is neither practiced nor held in esteem.

How can one survive—and even succeed—amid the chaos? Can the inanity be turned around into something useful?

You will find in this book the answers to those questions and road maps—practical steps—on how to get there. You can't just decide one day to be respectful and with the snap of fingers be done. No, it's work. But worthwhile work that can have a lasting effect on all your interactions and society at large.

You may skip around chapters, reading first what appeals to you. But please do go back and read every chapter as each contributes to the others and you will learn profound lessons and practical tips along the way.

While my books typically have been for a business audience—and this one *is* perfect for entrepreneurs to directors to CEOs—it also will resonate with anyone at any point in their life who wants to improve interpersonal communication and relate to others with authenticity. Isn't that all of us?

You will read of the experiences of a dozen-plus thought leaders in diverse areas such as education, hospitality, politics, nonprofit foundations, and for-profit industry. They will share their lessons on incorporating respectfulness into their work and personal lives. Their views are interspersed among the chapters; here they are alphabetically:

A Call for Respectfulness 3

- Alex von Bidder is a partner of the former Four Seasons restaurant in Manhattan, the place to be and be seen for business and cultural leaders. He will tell you what happened the day Jacqueline Onassis arrived without a reservation. He dishes his personal strategy for dealing with stressful situations gracefully.
- Dr. Miguel Cardona rose from an inner-city fourth-grade teacher fresh out of college to the 12th US Secretary of Education. Spanish was his first language; he learned English in kindergarten and talks about the lasting value of a supportive family and community. He describes ways respectfulness is taught in the classroom with students taking responsibility.
- Michael Dowling is the CEO emeritus of Northwell Health, the largest private health-care provider in New York and locations in Connecticut with more than 105,000 employees. He speaks of how he learned self-respect growing up in a rural village in Ireland and of his somewhat startling approach to ferret out disrespect in the workplace.
- Phil Gramm, the former US senator from Texas who brought his economic acuity to Washington, discusses what he thinks is needed to return respectfulness among the major political parties and within Congress.
- Sarah McArthur is an author and the editor in chief of *Leader to Leader*, the online journal for the Frances Hesselbein Leadership Forum at the University of Pittsburgh's Graduate School of Public and International Affairs. She reflects on profound lessons in respectfulness from Hesselbein, the former CEO of the Girl Scouts who brought the organization into the modern era and worked with management guru Peter Drucker.
- Betsy McCaughey was a lieutenant governor in the administration of Republican governor George Pataki and made a mark in health care with protocols for reducing patient infections. Now as a weekend news talk show host, she discloses how she deals with guests with whom she disagrees.

- Kelly McKenzie, an award-winning author from Vancouver, relates the challenges of handling disrespectful customers in retail where you can't just walk away.
- Stuart Muszynski established with his clinical psychologist wife, Dr. Susan Muszynski, the Values-in-Action Foundation, which now provides free curriculum to teach kindness in schools across all 50 states. He talks about what kids today think about the quality of respectfulness.
- Allia Zobel Nolan, the award-winning author of religious, children's, and adult books, often involving cats, talks about shifting social cues that can lead to awkward situations and how she handles them.
- Indra Nooyi is well-known for her leadership as the former president and CEO of PepsiCo and today a board member of high-profile corporations. She discusses how she fostered respectfulness in a multilayered environment at work and how the value of respectfulness has changed in society.
- MaryLou Pagano, the executive director of The Sheen Center for Thought and Culture in New York City, describes how she approaches respectfulness with her staff, performers, and patrons; each requires something different.
- Rabbi Arthur Schneier, a leader of the historic landmark Park East Synagogue in New York City and founder of the Appeal of Conscience Foundation, is widely respected as a humanitarian. He provides his views on respectfulness in religion and his interactions with world leaders.
- Sol Trujillo is an international business leader, having run communications networks in more than 30 countries. He describes the three points he sees in determining respectfulness.

All of these leaders talk about much more in the exploration of respectfulness in every facet of life. Do they think it's possible to consistently be respectful? Their answers might surprise you.

■ ■ ■

A Call for Respectfulness

We can agree that the atmosphere in society has to change. The foundation for that change is respect. To be respectful. In this book I will guide you into building respectfulness into your daily life, your workplace, civic institutions, society, our planet, humankind. I know this sounds lofty. But it's not woo-woo stuff, either. Respectfulness must emanate from you in all of your endeavors and interactions.

As Malala Yousafzai, the activist for girls' education in Pakistan who at 15 was shot by the Taliban while riding a school bus, urged, "We should all consider each other as human beings, and we should respect each other."[1] This is a powerful statement considering how she was treated.

Following the adage "you get what you give," when you live a life of respectfulness, you will gain respect.

Although children are taught in some cultures to "respect your elders," respect is not automatic. As with wisdom, respect does not necessarily come with age. It must be earned. And it also must be nurtured because, like your reputation, respect can be lost.

Respectfulness is a vitally important part of a functioning society. That is a lesson that must be taught—even drilled into—every new generation. A lesson that goes something like this: a good citizen has an obligation to extend respect to others and has the right to expect it in return. You don't necessarily have to like everyone you deal with, but you should treat them with at least a minimal level of respect.

What does that look like?

Respect is a word like *love* or *caring* that bears a positive connotation, but it can mean different things to different people.

As Aretha Franklin insisted in her anthem: "R-E-S-P-E-C-T, find out what it means to *me*!"[2]

■ ■ ■

Norman Cousins, the legendary figure in publishing circles who was editor in chief of the prestigious *Saturday Review* when I knew him, was instrumental in teaching me respectfulness. He did this by the example of how he interacted with people of all kinds. He showed me a way to handle others with ease, respect, and sophistication. I can never imagine Cousins insulting anyone. It just did not happen. If he were insulted, he took it with a smile and thanked the person for his comment. This unexpected response can be disarming.

The subtext of Cousins's lessons was that the "old rules" of good manners and ethical behavior never truly get old. That includes treating others with respect.

Does this seem easy? Maybe so when you are dealing with someone you like. But try it with someone whose political views are diametrically opposite yours. It gets harder to respect the person when their beliefs are abhorrent to you. Yet this is what is needed if we are ever going to repair our divided society.

The anthropologist Margaret Mead understood. "I have a respect for manners as such, they are a way of dealing with people you don't agree with or like," she said.[3]

Alex von Bidder, the manager of the storied former Four Seasons restaurant in Manhattan, said he thinks people don't know how to teach or follow the rules of etiquette anymore. And there *are* rules.

"It's like behavior exhibited at court," he explained. "For example, when going to Buckingham Palace, there will be a rehearsal, a walk through, a discussion on the proper way to address the king." You will read about von Bidder's methods for teaching manners—to children as well as adults—in Chapter 3.

Manners can be learned, but the tricky thing is they can vary from culture to culture and even circumstance to circumstance. What one person considers a show of good manners, another might see as insulting. Reading one handbook on etiquette won't suffice.

Today manners alone are an incomplete guide. At one time, a man holding a door open for a woman was considered chivalrous, exhibiting fine manners. Now the gesture could be interpreted as patronizing or belittling. How does one navigate social cues? What is a respectful way to respond—no matter what side of the door you face? You will find out in this book.

■ ■ ■

Let us examine what I consider the top five qualities that comprise being respectful. (Not that there are only five but starting with a number makes them easier to remember.)

> **5.** Listen to others—really listen—instead of thinking about what you'll say next.
> **4.** Understand that everyone has their own experiences and beliefs.
> **3.** Be courteous; help others see the good.
> **2.** Practice compassion; foster a sense of belonging.
> **1.** Acknowledge the dignity of human life, no matter one's station, culture, or preferences.

"It's not who you are, but how you act that garners respect," said Allia Zobel Nolan, the writer of more than 150 published books, many of them for children.

In future chapters, we will apply these top five into various settings, such as the workplace, institutions, and everyday interactions. We will even talk about how to argue effectively—and respectfully to yourself and the other person or perhaps persons.

■ ■ ■

A starting point to develop and demonstrate respectfulness is to first respect yourself. You cannot respect others if you do not respect yourself.

Paradoxically, gaining self-respect requires not looking to others for respect or validation. It is a quality that must come from within. Then, and only then, can it extend outward authentically.

The ancient Chinese philosopher Lao Tzu advised, "When you are content to be simply yourself and don't compare or compete, everybody will respect you."[4]

One way you can cultivate this sense of self-respect is through daily habits that involve using your time wisely, not being pulled in many directions according to what others want. Learn how to say no—at the right times. When you value your time, others will, too.

If you are someone who has said yes to others most of your life, then it can be hard to be someone who says no sometimes. You are wired to avoid disappointing someone else. But in the long run if you always put yourself second, you are the one who will end up disappointed. You will feel like you are missing out on what you really want to do.

"All relationships require a little give and take, but if getting someone to like you more makes you like yourself less, it's not worth the price," said Jefferson Fisher, the author of *The Next Conversation: Argue Less, Talk More*.[5]

"There's nothing wrong with pleasing people," he said. "Just make sure you're one of them."

Find and follow your purpose. What speaks to you, not what others say is right for you. When you are guided by your purpose, you'll see how parts of your life fit together; you are in the flow. You can tap into your creative energy—yes, it's there!

Sarah McArthur, editor in chief of *Leader to Leader*, uses a question posed by her mentor, Frances Hesselbein, to find purpose.

"What is it you see when you look out the window that is visible but not yet seen?" Hesselbein, the long-time CEO of the national Girl Scouts, would ask. She wasn't talking about squirrels!

It was an invitation, a direction, to "explore our deepest thoughts, concerns, fears and hopes for our society," McArthur said.[6]

Do you know your purpose? Are you honoring it—or waiting until some day when all conditions are perfect? Do not delay.

And even though this is obvious, it bears saying: take care of yourself. You cannot have self-respect if you neglect your physical, mental, and spiritual health. Keep learning. (Be sure to give yourself credit for learning by reading this book!)

Try not to take things personally, such as a perceived slight or an ugly comment on social media. Don't respond to emotional triggers—that's needlessly stressful and counterproductive. When you begin to control your reactions, you will be building self-respect.

The journalist writer Hunter S. Thompson noted the importance of self-respect. In his book *The Proud Highway* he wrote, "We shall all someday look back on our lives and see that, in spite of our company, we were alone the whole way. I do not say lonely—at least, not all the time—but essentially, and finally alone. This is what makes your self-respect so important, and I don't see how you can respect yourself if you must look in the hearts and minds of others for your happiness."[7]

Ground yourself; be authentic and sincere. From this solid space of self-respect, you can conduct your life with respectfulness for others.

■ ■ ■

When you live a life of respectfulness you are considerate of others. You pay attention. On the Fourth of July a good friend happened to be in a touristy candy store and during the routine transaction of paying the cashier, she thanked her for working a holiday. The cashier was truly surprised by this small gesture and appreciated being "seen" as a person and not merely a function. And you know what? My friend said she felt unexpectedly buoyant by the simple connection.

Meaningful conversation can be blocked by psychological barriers, for example, thinking that your comments would have no impact.

"Belonging is a fundamental human need virtually on par with eating and sleeping and yet previous research suggests that people often forgo opportunities to connect with others that would satisfy this need and thereby enhance both their own and others' well-being," write Michael Kardas, Amit Kumar, and Nicholas Epley in a 2021 article for the American Psychological Association.[8]

"Even the briefest engagements with others, from saying 'hello' to a barista to making eye contact with a passerby, can increase the sense of connection to others," they wrote, and yet people sometimes avoid even these easy ways to engage with others.

They can become reluctant to give compliments, express gratitude, or perform random acts of kindness. Why? Because, at least partly, people underestimate the positive impact their social behavior will have on others, they wrote.

"Misunderstanding how positively others value social interaction can create a barrier to engaging with others, thereby creating a systematic barrier to satisfying the basic human need for belonging."

I might add that it's easier to pull out your phone and scroll through email—anything—to avoid making small talk with a stranger. The ups and downs of small talk and the avoidance of it is a topic for Chapter 3.

■ ■ ■

In the workplace respectfulness requires cultivating a culture where people feel safe to express their opinions without retribution or being ignored. It requires deliberately seeking views that are different from your own, perhaps because of experiences, culture, or other factors.

"Be mindful and attentive," said international business leader Sol Trujillo. "Listen on a personal level. If you don't listen, the result is negative."

Phil Smith of Marathon Oil understood the power of words. He would select each word he spoke or wrote carefully and each word would carry meaning, the way in poetry every word must count. You never left his office without feeling something positive. He was not the head of Marathon, he was in the communication department. Nonetheless, he had influence, and people came to him. He listened.

There's a term called *active listening*, which is a way to let others be heard. And that's *not* just what they say with words. The unspoken words and body language must be noticed. In Chapter 5 we will describe the tools to employ for active listening. At its core is respectfulness for the other.

Individual respectfulness in the workplace can go far to foster a sense of belonging. Indra Nooyi, early in her executive leadership roles, would look around the conference table and not see herself. That is, she was the only woman and, being a native of India, the only immigrant in a seat. She tried to stay calm. I would say it is difficult to hold a respectful attitude in such circumstances. Many would probably talk louder or somehow command attention—not terribly productive. Nooyi approached the imbalance with hard work, innovative ideas, and listening. She rose to become the president and then CEO of PepsiCo for a dozen pivotal years; she was the first woman to lead a Fortune 50 company. During her tenure that extended to 2018, she was intent on reshaping the ubiquitous soda and snack company—Lay's potato chips were among the holdings—into a health-conscious and environmentally sensitive organization.[9] You will learn more about Nooyi's leadership style and how she cultivated a culture of respectfulness in Chapter 6.

■ ■ ■

Maybe when you were a kid your mother told you to "live and let live." This means more than not stepping on ants, though that's a good admonishment, too. Recognize that others have the right to live their lives according to their beliefs, even if it means, say, they voted for a candidate you deem unworthy.

"That principle of respecting people or treating people the way you want to be treated doesn't go away because you ideologically are different than me," said Miguel Cardona, the former US Secretary of Education. The principle should remain no matter the circumstances.

It can be hard to find a kernel of respect for someone who denigrates or shames or works for opposing goals. But try. You can't be open-minded only when people think as you do.

"It's harder, definitely harder," said cable news and analysis show host Betsy McCaughey, "but life is long and if you take the long view, civility is the better course of action."

Different viewpoints and opinions can lead to arguments, sometimes loud, sometimes followed by the silent treatment. No one feels good. We will talk in detail in Chapter 7 about strategies for navigating through disagreements—while remaining true to yourself.

We will talk about communication and how it can get distorted in the digital age and gain outsized influence in social media.

■ ■ ■

Social media has its positives, but it is not to be trusted as a reliable source of fact or truth.

A quote has been going around the internet for quite a while attributed to the actress Meryl Streep. In part it says,

> I have no patience for cynicism, excessive criticism and demands of any nature. I lost the will to please those who do not like me, to love those who do not love me and to smile at those who do not want to smile at me.
>
> I no longer spend a single minute on those who lie or want to manipulate. I decided not to coexist anymore with pretense, hypocrisy, dishonesty and cheap praise. I do not tolerate selective erudition nor academic arrogance. I do not adjust either to popular gossiping. I hate conflict and comparisons. I believe in a world of opposites and that's why I avoid people with rigid and inflexible personalities.[10]

That could sound like her, right? (Or our perceptions of what a respected actress would say.)

The trouble is, she didn't say any of that; she never made that statement. Yet it has circulated around the internet for more than 10 years—with her photo, making it more believable.

Do you know who did say those words? José Micard Teixeira, a Portuguese life coach/self-help guru, according to Snopes.com, a reputable fact-checking site.[11]

"Popular quotations need famous mouths, history has proved time and again: If you want people to pay attention to a statement, the odds that they will do so are greatly enhanced if those words seemingly issued from the mind and lips of someone they know and respect," Snopes reported.

Here's how the inaccuracy happened, according to Snopes: "As far as we can tell, the earliest Facebook reposting of Teixeira's words that incorrectly credited them to Meryl Streep occurred on the page of Tuncluer Textiles on 15 July 2014, and the quote went viral in that form after being combined with a photograph of Meryl

Streep and published on the Romanian-language "Ioadicaeu's Blog" on 31 July 2014."

Teixeira tried to set the record straight, but the misattributed quote persists.

This is a lesson in how even something that is not negative can be false and take on a life of its own. You cannot believe everything you read in social media.

"Twitter is a platform consecrated to the eternal pie fight—to the purposes of protest, complaint, and particularly punishment—where nobody is special and nobody is invulnerable," wrote Tom Junod of the site now called X in the December 2019 issue of *The Atlantic* magazine.[12] His article, "My Friend Mister Rogers," was about the unlikely friendship between the children's television show host and the investigative reporter after the movie "Won't You Be My Neighbor?" with Tom Hanks playing Fred Rogers came out.

■ ■ ■

The potentially harmful effect of social media on children is particularly alarming.

"There are increasing concerns among researchers, parents and caregivers, young people, healthcare experts, and others about the impact of social media on youth mental health," wrote then Surgeon General Vivek Murthy in a 2023 advisory titled "Social Media and Youth Mental Health."[13]

Social media use by youth is nearly universal. "Up to 95% of youth ages 13–17 report using a social media platform, with more than a third saying they use social media 'almost constantly,'" the report states. Age 13 is commonly the required minimum age used by social media platforms in the United States, but nearly 40% of children ages 8–12 use social media, the report found.

It is not all negative, but not enough research has been conducted to determine the extent of impact, whether beneficial or detrimental. However, early indications of troubling symptoms include depression and anxiety.

Digital social interactions discourage in-person connectedness and can lead to feelings of isolation.

For example, the report stated, "How does social comparison affect one's sense of life satisfaction and in-person relationships? How does the use of social media, including specific designs and features, relate to dopamine pathways involved in motivation, reward, and addiction?"

Recommendations for what policymakers and tech companies can do are included in the 25-page advisory. I find the ones for individuals helpful for parents and families.

Among them: "Create tech-free zones and encourage children to foster in-person friendships." Keep family mealtimes device-free to encourage two-way conversation. Restrict the use of phones, tablets, and computers for at least one hour before bedtime as their use can interfere with sleep.

Adults would do well to model responsible social behavior as children learn by example. Limit your use. Put down your phone—better yet, put it away—when talking with children. Give them your full attention.

"Help your child develop social skills and nurture his or her in-person relationships by encouraging unstructured and offline connections with others and making unplugged interactions a daily priority," the report recommends.

Young adults, those under the age of 30, also appear to be affected by social changes.

In a 2025 article in *The Atlantic* titled "Why Are Young People Everywhere Unhappy?," Arthur C. Brooks cites various studies pointing to the "falling happiness of young adults in America."[14]

Though a single cause is not determined, Brooks lists three actions that could be taken immediately to help young adults—or anyone—flourish now.

1. Put close relationships with family and friends before virtually everything else. Where possible, avoid using technological platforms for interactions with these loved ones; focus on face-to-face contact. Humans are made to relate to one another in person.
2. Consider how you might develop your inner life ... transcend the daily grind and find purpose and meaning.
3. Material comforts are great, but they're no substitute for what your heart truly needs. Money can't buy happiness; only meaning can give you that.

Michael Dowling, the CEO emeritus of Northwell Health, the largest private health-care provider in New York with a network that includes Western Connecticut, is greatly concerned about the negative health effects of social media.

It leads, he said, to "an extraordinary increase in anxiety, depression and suicide among the young. And there's a direct correlation between social media and that. But if you have a healthy community, people respect one another; people work together; people help one another. You create a kind of positive family atmosphere."

One path to getting kids away from their screens, interacting with others, and learning life skills is through sports.

Little League has a phrase for parents called *honoring the game*.[15] The tenets can be remembered through the acronym ROOTS: respect for rules, opponents, officials, teammates, and self.

"You don't bend the Rules to win. You understand that a worthy Opponent helps you to play to your highest potential. You respect Officials even when you disagree with their calls. You refuse to do anything that embarrasses your Teammates. Even if others fail to live up to these standards, you live up to the standards you set for your Self."

Similarly, Pop Warner Football promotes respect through positive conduct, respect for officials, respect for the game—such as not trying to disrupt the competition by throwing objects onto the field—and respect for your opponent, the players, coaches, and fans.[16]

Respect

Some of the greatest lessons happen in sports. There's a statue in Brooklyn, New York, of baseball player Pee Wee Reese with his arm around Jackie Robinson depicting one of the most famous and celebrated moments in baseball history. It is a centerpiece of Ken Burns's documentary *Baseball*.[17] It's often referred to simply as the embrace, that moment when Reese put his arm around the shoulders of his teammate Robinson as racist catcalls descended from the stands in Kansas City in 1947. Racism wasn't just in Kansas City for the first Black major league baseball player. Robinson demonstrated grace and Reese showed courage—and respect.

A few months later, the second Black man in major league baseball, Larry Doby, joined the Cleveland Indians. Looking back on his career, he said, "The only thing I ask for you or any person is respect for a human being. If you don't want to accept me as a human being, I'll see you later."

■ ■ ■

Could you be a Pee Wee Reese and stand up for others? If not, the negative atmosphere in the public realm is endorsed whether by those actively joining in to denigrate the "other," for example, or by passively ignoring the culture of mean spiritedness. Either way, we are complicit. Either way, we have the agency to change and instill respectfulness for all.

Indra Nooyi, the former CEO of PepsiCo, said people should call out bad behavior. "When there is no standard for what is good behavior or not, each person defines their own good behavior and bad behavior."

Society has lost its moral compass when it is up to the individual to define "good" or "bad." One result is that autocracy can take hold. We can do better.

Respectfulness, to others and in yourself, is rooted in values such as trust, honesty, and integrity that also must be cultivated.

Treating others respectfully has life-changing consequences. It will take work, but it's well within the reach of us all. And society will be the better.

I am an optimist. Yes, I believe you can succeed in the world disorder; you can transcend the inane and create meaning. Will this be easy? Of course not. But it is possible. It is worthwhile. Let us begin.

Think About It

1. What value do you give the quality of respectfulness in your life?
2. This week make a brief, but meaningful, connection with someone you don't know very well. Maybe it's a grocery clerk: make eye contact and say something sincere and specific, such as "Thank you for handling my eggs so carefully."
3. Observe the reaction to your comment. What was your reaction; how did that make you feel?

CHAPTER 2

Is Respectfulness Truly Possible in the Age of Retribution?

Respect was invented to cover the empty place where love should be.

– Leo Tolstoy, *Anna Karenina*

Society has changed greatly in the past few decades—so much so that it's not a stretch to call the changes cataclysmic. Technology has exploded, enabling instant communication and news as it's happening, though the sources and slants can be difficult to discern. It has allowed autonomy in social media posts that contributes to nastiness, name-calling, and worse. And the proliferation of artificial intelligence will have profound effects on industry and human interactions with consequences yet to be discovered. The question must be asked: Has the value of respectfulness endured or been eroded? Is respectfulness truly possible in these times of retribution, denigration, and disregard of the other?

Thought leader Stuart Muszynski didn't hesitate when he answered my question with this assessment—no, not possible. "I struggle with this idea of respect," he said. "I think that ship has sailed."

Muszynski knows young people. He and Dr. Susan Muszynski, who is a clinical psychologist and his wife, in 1994 cofounded Values-in-Action,[1] an Ohio-based nonprofit that provides social-emotional and character education programs to schools. The organization has grown to now reach more than 9,000 schools and had 4,900 participating schools across all 50 states in 2024.

> *Stuart Muszynski is the cofounder, president, and CEO of the Values-in-Action Foundation. His background in business includes marketing and insurance consulting specializing in areas such as turnarounds and economic development.*
>
> *He cofounded Project Love, Remember the Children Foundation, with his wife, Susan Muszynski, PhD, in 1994. Stuart Muszynski is the author of* Searching for Values: A Grandmother and Grandson and the Discovery of Goodness *as well as numerous articles dealing with education, character, and values.*
>
> *Among his recognitions are the National Cyberbully Day Award in 2011 and the Outstanding Community Leader Award from the National Sales and Marketing Executives in 2021.*

About 20 years ago they noticed a cultural shift: "I'll respect you if you respect me first," led by the millennials. The shift started with reality television and the early version was hardly respectful.

"Then there was a social media wave that began about 15 years ago. And social media is anything but respectful.

"So it's hard to say to anybody, especially to young people today, to respect your elders, respect your teachers, respect people with authority. Also, it's because we have seen people in authority—police, clergy, athletes—not being respectful.

"So I struggle with this idea," he said. But that does not mean hope for civility is lost.

"What I don't struggle with is the idea of kindness," Muszynski offered. "At the same time we saw respect diminish in our schools, we saw a desire for kindness growing."

Muszynski said he thinks we need to promote and encourage kindness and then respect will follow.

Is Respectfulness Truly Possible in the Age of Retribution?

How is that done? One way is talk about how we all feel when kindness is given to us. It can be as simple as a smile. Talk about kindness in school, business, nonprofits, churches, synagogues, and mosques. Describe what that looks like. When everybody starts talking about kindness—and acts accordingly—then respect and civility will be the natural results. This is what Muszynski believes.

"But it can't go the other way. You just can't go back and say, 'Respect your elders.' There's been a very serious cultural shift in our nation and it continues to be exacerbated by our media and exacerbated by our politics," he said.

We are not seeing respectful role modeling in those areas. Politicians on the national level are accused of caring more about staying on the good side of the executive administration than standing up for their constituents.

You need to have a high sense of moral views to tell someone to be respectful to a person who is not acting respectfully.

The faith-based Golden Rule—Do unto others as you would have them do unto you—is, unfortunately, a passé term, Muszynski said. "What kids understand and would much rather say is, 'What goes around, comes around.'"

Maybe that phrase is not as elegant, but the message comes across. If you are kind, people will be kind to you. If you are respectful, people will be respectful to you. If you are mean and nasty, guess what? People will be mean and nasty to you.

And it seems that's the kind of behavior—mean and nasty—that is cheered on these days, particularly on social media.

Leaders need to show that society is better when people are considerate of each other; at the very least they should be tolerant.

The foundation created by the Muszynskis aims to change the dynamic, starting with students. It's not that adults are hopeless cases; it's that change can be lasting if started with younger generations.

The Values-in-Action Foundation offers free programs to schools that, among other things, provide skills and tools to make positive decisions and to build communities of kindness and caring.

For example, the foundation has a workforce training program, developed with the Auburn Career Center, that prepares workforce-oriented 11th- and 12th-grade students with skills needed for employment. Those skills include responsibility, ethics, integrity, and kindness, plus self-awareness and resiliency.

The training is based on methodology the foundation had used in the Cleveland, Ohio, metropolitan school system, which saw a 47% graduation rate among some of the most at-risk students nearly double to 93%.

You will see more about Values-in-Action in the schools and communities in Chapter 8. The greatest challenge with encouraging kindness among kids might surprise you.

"From time to time, some kids have said, 'You know what? If everybody were nice, it would be pretty boring,'" Muszynski said. Kids are used to the edginess of video games, YouTube, and TikTok. Kindness? Where's the excitement?

His comeback to kind-is-boring (I can just see the eyerolls) is to ask them whether they like getting together with cousins, with family. That's not boring, right? It takes the wind out of their sails, is how he put it. From there, they can talk about creating a world that's kind and respectful.

■ ■ ■

If only "kind and respectful" were encouraged by society these days as much as sensationalism and attention.

Betsy McCaughey sees the push for sensationalism up close in her profession, even as she repels it. She is a host on *Wake Up America Weekend*, which is broadcast on the cable channel Newsmax.

"A PR (public relations) person with whom I was talking earlier said, 'What you need is a good fight on the radio or television,'" she told me. "Obviously, the professionals are advising just the opposite" of civility.

That's not for her.

"I think it's important to develop a reputation for civility," she said. "I've never attacked on the air. I've been attacked myself many times and I will always stand up for myself, of course, but I don't think most viewers really like a knockdown, drag-out, fight on the air. They want to hear both viewpoints."

Betsy McCaughey is a host of a cable television news and analysis show, Wake Up America Weekend, *a health policy expert, and former lieutenant governor of New York State in the administration of George Pataki. In 2004, she founded the Committee to Reduce Infection Deaths, a nationwide educational campaign to stop hospital-acquired infections, which led to legislation in more than 25 states for public reporting of infection rates to improve patient safety.*

Dr. McCaughey is the author of more than 100 scholarly and popular articles on health policy, infection, medical innovation, the economics of aging, and Medicare. Her writings have appeared in the New York Times, The Wall Street Journal, New Republic, *and many other national publications. She writes a regular column for the* New York Post.

She has taught at Vassar College and Columbia University, and produced prize-winning studies while at two think tanks: the Manhattan Institute and later the Hudson Institute.

Dr. McCaughey earned her PhD in constitutional history. She is the author of two books on that subject: From Loyalist to Founding Father, *winner of the Bancroft Dissertation Award, and* Government by Choice. *She also chaired a national commission on reforming the Electoral College in 1992, wrote its report, "Electing the President," and testified before Congress on the subject.*

Respect

I've known Betsy for about 25 years; she has an office in New York City. She is a person who can command to see virtually anybody in the media. Every summer she has a lunch in the country and everybody shows up. It's a great experience.

She has a big personality. By that I mean she's gregarious and laughs a lot. When she says something you listen because you realize she's got all this background and experience.

I asked her about the challenge of being respectful in these times of rancor and divisiveness.

"Well, I feel I'm particularly practiced at it now because I'm a host of a television show," she said. "When I invite guests on, they're doing me a huge favor and the audience a huge favor by taking the time to appear. And I often have guests whose viewpoints are very unlike mine.

"But I have to be respectful because, after all, they're giving me their time; they're giving me their thoughts. And I feel that by showing respect, it also encourages the audience to give the guests' ideas and viewpoints a second thought."

She said it's the same when she's interviewing people for the columns she writes for the *New York Post*.

"I'm already indebted to them for sharing their thoughts and it encourages me to give consideration to the viewpoints, even though I may reflexively disagree with them."

I've read her columns and find them well-researched and well-reasoned, even if one disagrees with her position. She pulls no punches but is not retaliatory or mean.

Yet, in politics there's "often a premium put on being pugnacious, nasty," she noted.

"That's just the way it is. Look at how much fame Elise Stefanik, the Congress[person] from upstate New York, has gained by her attacks on the president of Harvard."

During a December 5, 2023, Congressional hearing on "Holding Campus Leaders Accountable and Confronting Antisemitism," Stefanik told Harvard University President Claudine Gay her answers were "unacceptable" and she should resign.[2] Less than a month later, Gay, the first Black president of Harvard, did resign.

McCaughey said she agreed with Stefanik's viewpoint, but not the way she went about expressing it.

"You know, I don't think she would have won all this acclaim even from the president had she been mild mannered in her questioning," she said. "So it's unfortunate that civility is seldom rewarded in the political arena."

Though Stefanik is a Republican, McCaughey said she could as easily refer to Democrats "from all over the country who have been extremely nasty in the political arena.

"That ability to fight with words is often very well rewarded."

Former US Sen. Phil Gramm sees what he calls a "breakdown of respect" in the Senate. The protocol had been based on respecting other members, regardless of party, but he said that in debate today politicians say things they couldn't have gotten away with in earlier years.

Michael Dowling, the CEO emeritus of Northwell Health, has seen the culture shift in a matter of years.

"I spent 12 years in government as one of the top guys for Governor [Mario] Cuomo in New York State," he said. He had been Cuomo's state director of Health, Education, and Human Services and deputy secretary and was also commissioner of the New York State Department of Social Services.

"And the difference between then and now is that I was on the Democratic side and some of my best friends were Republican.

"Even though we argued every day on issues, we respected each other and hung out together at night. We never became disagreeable because we had disagreed."

But now a frequently tossed around word is *lunatic*, he said.

"'The lunatic left wing,' 'the lunatic fringe'—I mean, that's not decent. That language demonstrates the kind of person you are."

The challenge is how to turn that environment around and instead reward civility and respectfulness, not only in politics but also any endeavor.

■ ■ ■

The power of words was reflected in Pope Leo XIV's first audience with news outlets days after being elected to one of the highest positions in the world.[3]

"Let us disarm communication of all prejudice and resentment, fanaticism and even hatred; let us free it from aggression," Leo told more than 1,000 journalists who were gathered in an auditorium on May 12, 2025.

The new pope spoke of the need for people to be informed so they can make sound decisions, a role that reputable media should fulfill, and of "the precious gift of free speech and of the press."

"We do not need loud, forceful communication but rather communication that is capable of listening," he added. He renewed calls for a more peaceful world.

Maybe there is hope when this is the view of a prominent moral leader.

Sarah McArthur, the editor in chief of *Leader to Leader*, believes it is "absolutely" possible to be respectful in all instances, but—the catch is—it is incredibly difficult.

"That to me is the character-building part. If I can be constantly building my character and strengthening my character as I can find a way to be respectful in all situations, all conversations. It's not easy, it's definitely not easy," she said, speaking of responding to someone who is disrespectful to you. "That's a big reason why a lot of people probably aren't respectful. It is so much easier to not be—you don't have to think, you don't have to listen."

McArthur has a lot more to say about respectfulness, which you will read elsewhere in this book, including Chapter 7.

Respectfulness is put to the test when confronted with the opposite: disrespect. Could respectfulness whither if not tended or deemed a valuable quality in society? Could it be stamped out when those in power choose to act with coercion instead of diplomacy? Is it on its last gasp when the mantra is everyone for themselves?

We need to step away from our present-day miasma to seek answers.

■ ■ ■

Is Respectfulness Truly Possible in the Age of Retribution?   27

What does it mean to respect someone or something? When trying to understand a complex concept, it is useful to look at the word's etymology. The word *respect* is from the Latin *respectus*, which means regard with the sense of looking back.

The word has been around a long time. One of the earliest known uses is in the Middle English period (1150–1500). The *Oxford English Dictionary (OED)* notes the word *respect* was used as a noun before 1398.[4]

There are 25 meanings listed in *OED*'s entry for the noun *respect*, 15 of which it labels obsolete. It seems we can't even agree on how to pronounce the word: ruh-SPECKT or ree-SPECKT.

Not surprisingly, therefore, the concept of respect raises questions. Is it a "mode of behavior, a form of treatment, a kind of valuing, a type of attention, a motive, an attitude, a feeling, a tribute, a principle, a duty, an entitlement, a moral virtue, an epistemic virtue"? These questions are posed in the *Stanford Encyclopedia of Philosophy*.[5] Are there different kinds or different levels of respect? Another noted question is, "How is respect similar to, different from or connected with esteem, honor, love, awe, reverence, recognition, toleration, dignity, contempt, indifference, discounting, denigration, and so on?"

The concept can have meanings of various weights and different modes of conduct. For example, there is an institutional respect, such as standing when a judge enters or leaves the courtroom. Such a show of respect is not voluntary, it is synonymous with obeying rules, such as "respecting" the speed limit. Or respect could be more like a tribute, such as saluting your country's flag or placing your hand over your heart when the national anthem is played.

When respect means to think highly of someone, to hold them in esteem, it is a deliberate response, a choice, not an order.

German philosopher Immanuel Kant in the eighteenth century argued that all people should be treated with respect simply because they are people with absolute dignity. Imagine how radical that must have sounded at the time! Respect was not accorded by position, class, or wealth, but was a fundamental moral obligation owed to all individuals on the basis of being rational beings.[6]

Kant was the first major Western philosopher to place respect for the individual at the center of moral theory. In more recent times, some have extended that respect for individuals to animals, nature, or the environment.

Kant said, "Every man is to be respected as an absolute end in himself; and it is a crime against the dignity that belongs to him as a human being, to use him as a mere means for some external purpose."

Never treat others as if they have little or no worth compared to ourselves, Kant said, or their only value is their usefulness to us. That would be shameful indeed.

What happens when not all are thought of as worthy of respect, when some are considered to have greater moral worth? The result is at the core of racism, sexism, bigotry.

Perhaps you have heard of Kant's categorial imperative: moral commands all must follow, regardless of their desires or extenuating circumstances; these imperatives are binding on everyone. The supreme principle of morality commands that our actions express respect for people, who are unconditionally valuable. I think of this as similar to the unconditional love of a parent for their child.

Respectfulness does not mean that anything goes, however. Autonomy and agency are embedded, that is, individuals are encouraged to make their own decisions, take responsibility for their actions, and control their lives.

Respectfulness means seeing each person as a distinctive individual with differences as well as commonalities.

Respect and its twin, self-respect, are therefore personally, socially, and morally important.

■ ■ ■

What can we extract from this philosophical discussion for the purposes of this book? What does it mean in your life?

Is Respectfulness Truly Possible in the Age of Retribution?

Kant expanded the Golden Rule of "Do unto others as you would have them do unto you" to act as you would want everyone to act toward *all* other people. Act as though respectfulness to the individual were a universal law governing behavior.

As disruptive as such thoughts were in the eighteenth century, in this age is true respectfulness possible, can it thrive when it is not valued?

I would like to think that it is possible in an authentic way, though as Sarah McArthur noted it is not easy to respond respectfully when one is confronted with disrespect. Respectfulness is a value, an attitude, that must be encouraged and nourished in one's home, workplace, and society. Work is necessary to keep the flame of respect burning.

It would seem facile to say that the world would be a better place if we have respect for each other, but it is true. "That doesn't necessarily mean that everyone has to get along or agree all the time," McArthur said. "Respect for the majority is part of the democratic process and we can have respect for our disagreement."

Can you disagree respectfully? Without shouting (not just in person but also—and maybe most especially—in social media communication), without insisting that you are obviously right and the other is terribly wrong, without gleefully piling on?

Civility means respecting the other person's point of view, no matter how wide of mark, bizarre, or even ignorant you may think it is. Expressing contempt, disdain, or ridicule for an opposing point of view will never convince the other to see things your way. (I wrote about civility in a paper for my clients a while back.[7])

Don't question motives—instead, discuss policies. Listen closely and ask questions. Don't degrade the other; explain your position and reasoning.

Too many today take their cues from a polarizing, attack-oriented political culture, as we have seen earlier in this chapter. But you can help your adversaries understand they are as reasonable, thoughtful, and perhaps as smart as you are, but simply off base on a particular issue, whatever it may be. You might even change a few minds in the process.

Hard as it may be, try using responses such as "I understand why you hold that position … . There may be merit in what you say … . I respect your beliefs … . Let's discuss an alternative." You get the idea.

Sometimes friends, associates, or family members may be stressed and under pressure and say things totally out of character. Let them be; let them sound off.

We all stumble now and then and could say something we would later regret. Keep that in mind and don't overreact if insulted. If you strike back, you will probably exacerbate an already tense situation.

Snark is a trendy term that defines a tone of teasing, snide, subtle abuse, nasty and knowing, that is just unnecessary. But it is everywhere these days. Snark attempts to annihilate someone's reputation. Snarkers like to think they are witty, but mostly they are exposing the seethe and snarl of an unhappy moment, releasing savage gossip, bad feeling, and forced laughter. Indeed, some feel that the lowest, most insinuating and insulting side wins the day.

When confronted by a snarker, you could just walk away—or click away—or say "Is it that bad?" to dismiss the offender.

Snarkiness and respectfulness are opposites. You know which one to cultivate.

Marcus Aurelius advised, "The best revenge is not to be like your enemy."[8]

■ ■ ■

While the anonymity with much of social media has allowed nastiness and disrespect to flourish, it also has fed a sense of social isolation. People engage with a screen, less so with each other in person. Respectfulness falls by the wayside.

An epidemic of loneliness is what Dr. Vivek Murthy labeled it when he was the US Surgeon General. His 2023 advisory is as alarming as the phrase "epidemic of loneliness."[9]

Is Respectfulness Truly Possible in the Age of Retribution?

He pointed to the need for building more connected lives and a more connected society. "If we fail to do so, we will pay an ever-increasing price in the form of our individual and collective health and well-being," he wrote in the advisory. "And we will continue to splinter and divide until we can no longer stand as a community or a country. Instead of coming together to take on the great challenges before us, we will further retreat to our corners—angry, sick, and alone."

Loneliness is more than just a bad feeling—it harms the health of both the individual and society, he wrote. It is associated with a 29% greater risk of cardiovascular disease, a 32% increase in the risk of stroke, and a whopping 50% increase in the risk for older people to develop dementia; it can even lead to an early death.

One might wonder whether the COVID-19 pandemic influenced the loneliness, but even before the pandemic about half of US adults reported measurable loneliness. The epidemic is felt around the world, not just in the United States.

"In the last few decades, we've just lived through a dramatic pace of change. We move more, we change jobs more often, we are living with technology that has profoundly changed how we interact with each other and how we talk to each other," Murthy told NPR in a 2023 segment of *All Things Considered*[10] after issuing his advisory.

Although across all age groups people are spending less time with each other in person than 20 years ago, I find it particularly alarming that it is most pronounced in young people, aged 15–24, who had 70% less social interaction with their friends.

"And the harmful consequences of a society that lacks social connection can be felt in our schools, workplaces, and civic organizations, where performance, productivity, and engagement are diminished," Murthy wrote.

Among the harmful consequences, I would add, is a disregard for respectfulness. The Surgeon General's advisory included ways to build more connected lives and a more connected society.

Among them are strengthening social infrastructure, which includes public gathering places such as parks and libraries, and cultivating what he calls a *culture of connection*. Government policies and programs are needed but can't solve everything. Individuals also are responsible for creating a culture of connection.

Some people might think the epidemic of loneliness doesn't apply to them because they have a lot of friends. But it could—think about it honestly.

"You can feel lonely even if you have a lot of people around you, because loneliness is about the quality of your connections," Murthy said.

Here is his educated advice in the advisory:

"Each of us can start now, in our own lives, by strengthening our connections and relationships. Our individual relationships are an untapped resource—a source of healing hiding in plain sight. They can help us live healthier, more productive, and more fulfilled lives."

He listed 12 concrete recommendations for what individuals can do. They include "Seek out opportunities to serve and support others"; "Be responsive, supportive, and practice gratitude"; and "Participate in social and community groups."

This one, in particular, should be amplified: "Reflect the core values of connection in how you approach others in conversation and through the actions you take. Key questions to ask yourself when considering your interactions with others include 'How might kindness change this situation? What would it look like to treat others with respect?'"

Start now, Murthy urged. "Answer that phone call from a friend. Make time to share a meal. Listen without the distraction of your phone. Perform an act of service. Express yourself authentically. The keys to human connection are simple, but extraordinarily powerful."

■ ■ ■

Looking at personal disconnection from each other through the prism of profound loneliness can help us understand, in part, the roots of rancor. But there comes a time when one must stand up for instead treating each other with respectfulness. Consider it an obligation for a better society. And what it takes is a strong moral character.

One of the finest examples was shown to us by Fred Rogers, of all people. The year was 1969 and though the federal Civil Rights Act had passed five years earlier, segregation and distrust still existed. Racial tensions were rising; Dr. Martin Luther King Jr. had been assassinated the year before.

"Black citizens were still not embraced as equal participants in public life," Sara Kettler wrote in an article for the website Biography.[11] "This status was reflected at many community pools across the country, with white people preventing Black people from sharing the water with them."

I hope this feels unthinkable nowadays. Fred Rogers challenged the racism, not in a lecture but by example. In a May 6 episode that year of his children's television show *Mister Rogers' Neighborhood*, he invited a Black character, Police Officer Clemmons, to cool his feet with him in a plastic wading pool.

At first Officer Clemmons declined, saying he didn't have a towel to dry his feet; Mr. Rogers replied that they could share his.

"When Clemmons sat down and placed his feet in the water, right next to Rogers, the two men broke a well-known color barrier," Kettler wrote. It was a low-key, but powerful, depiction of friendship.

"It was a definite call to social action on Fred's part," François Clemmons (that was his real name) in 2018 told a reporter for vtdigger, a Vermont news website.[12] "That was his way of speaking about race relations in America."

In 2018 the blockbuster documentary *Won't You Be My Neighbor?* starring Tom Hanks as Fred Rogers drew fresh attention to the work of Rogers, who had died in 2003.

"The most radical thing about him was his unwavering commitment to the value of kindness in the face of the world that could seem intent on devising new ways to be mean," reviewer A. O. Scott wrote in the *New York Times* about the movie.[13]

Rogers' commitment to kindness was ubiquitous, not just part of his television persona.

Fred Rogers delivered the commencement address at the University of Connecticut in 1991 to a packed Gampel Pavilion that hushed when he spoke.

"We don't always succeed in what we try," he said to the graduates and audience, many of whom grew up watching his show, "but I think you'll find it's a willingness to keep trying that matters most."[14]

He received a thunderous standing ovation.

Rogers showed that respectfulness actually can coexist in a broken society. But it takes individual moral courage to make it happen. He asked the college graduates, "How will you help the children in your life to grow and develop into confident, helpful adults?"

■ ■ ■

Fred Rogers and Stuart Muszynski are right in that planting the seeds of kindness is a good way to start fostering the value of respectfulness.

The messaging of anything goes with political leaders in order to accomplish their goals has to change, Muszynski said; the counterbalance is kindness. "If society leads with kindness, they will be fast followers.

"Research shows that people will respond to kindness with kindness. We all have the kindness gene and all have the meanness gene. It is up to influencers to make the right one come out."

Fred Rogers emphasized the importance of kindness this way. "There are three ways to ultimate success," he said. "The first way is to be kind. The second way is to be kind. The third way is to be kind."

Think About It

1. Do you think respect is possible in these times or has that ship sailed?
2. Consider how to make kindness a valued action.
3. Do you agree with Immanuel Kant that everyone deserves respect by the very fact that they are human? How does this translate into your relationships?

CHAPTER 3

What's in It for Me?

Show respect to all people but grovel to none.
— Tecumseh

Kelly McKenzie was helping out at her mother's Asian antiques and collectibles boutique for what she thought would be an after-college summer job. FROG was a mostly high-end destination founded and operated by the strong-willed Frankie Robinson in Vancouver. McKenzie had a lot to learn. One day when she was alone tending the shop a customer became belligerent.

"His face infused with anger, he spewed saliva, and stamped his feet while demanding a ridiculous discount on a pair of antique baskets," McKenzie recounted. "When I refused to lower the price, explaining they were already offered at a large discount, he insisted I call my boss. She'd see his side and 'set me straight.'"

We've all heard that in business the customer is always right. But what about when the customer is blatantly rude?

McKenzie was annoyed with the disrespect shown to her, but even more to the carefully curated inventory.

"It was all I could do to not throw him out of the shop," she said. "But then I realized I shouldn't lower myself to his level. I was the better person. I should rise above it.

> *Kelly McKenzie, is a Canadian writer who has been published in various anthologies and newspapers.*
>
> *Her coming-of-age memoir,* Never, Never, Hardly Ever—A Mother/Daughter Story of Antiques and Antics, *is a behind-the-scenes look at the art of selling antiques in a women-led business. Having worked at her mother's successful Vancouver Asian antiques store for over a decade, McKenzie is well versed in all aspects of respectfulness.*
>
> *Shortlisted for the Whistler Independent Book Awards,* Never, Never, Hardly Ever *was also acknowledged as one of the best coming-of-age books by the fourth Annual Zibby Awards.*

"So I called Mom, as he insisted, and explained the situation in matter-of-fact terms. When I shared with the customer how she agreed with me, he stomped out of the shop." He was unaware that McKenzie was holding down the phone's disconnect button. The call never went through. She outsmarted him.

When disrespect manifests into bullying, you need to know how to handle the situation while maintaining your own sense of respect. This chapter will share some strategies that can be used.

McKenzie wrote her coming-of-age memoir—the job for the summer turned into a decade—and the cast of characters who came into the shop in *Never, Never Hardly Ever*,[1] published in 2024. She learned to deal with her quirk-magnet mother and to diffuse difficult situations with humor.

■ ■ ■

The title of this chapter, "What's in It for Me?," might seem like the antithesis of respectfulness. Shouldn't living your life with a respectful attitude be reward enough? No one should act respectfully only to get something out of it.

What's in It for Me?

Yes, but let's face it: abstracts can use some concrete support. Benefits motivate. We're human. Think of it this way: no matter how altruistic you are, when you look at a group photo, who is the first person you check out? Yourself, of course! It's only natural.

So in this chapter you will read of the personal benefits of respectfulness. Here's a start:

- Improve relationships
- Strengthen professional connections
- Ease stress

■ ■ ■

Alex von Bidder believes that being respectful is connected to manners, a direct link like honey to bees. "They go hand in hand" is the way he describes it.

Von Bidder was an owner of the iconic Four Seasons Restaurant, part of the Seagram Building, a New York City official landmark just off Park Avenue in midtown Manhattan. The interior designed by the renowned Philip Johnson featured five dining rooms, including balconies, in two main areas: the Grill Room and the Pool Room. Yes, that room featured an actual 20-by-20-foot white marble pool with corners anchored by huge fig tree planters. A Pablo Picasso curtain, part of a tapestry for the Ballets Russes, graced the foyer; brass sculptures abounded. Picture a mid-century modern vibe where 485 diners could be seated at once and served with silver platters.

> *Alex von Bidder, a native of Switzerland, was a partner and manager of the famed Four Seasons restaurant in Manhattan for more than 40 years. He coauthored* The Four Seasons: A History of America's Premier Restaurant *and the children's book* Wiggins Learns His Manners at the Four Seasons Restaurant.
>
> *(continued)*

> *He has taught manners at New York University, lectured at Cornell University, and cofounded the New York Mankind Project community.*
>
> *Von Bidder has been a trustee of the Tibet House US, a Tibetan culture and arts preservation center, and is chairman of the Advisory Committee of Rancho LaPuerta, a wellness resort and spa in Mexico.*
>
> *He is a certified yoga instructor and a meditation practitioner.*

For more than five decades the Four Seasons was *the* place to go for power lunches, birthday and anniversary dinners, and private events. It was where celebrities, politicians, and notables went to see and be seen. I always appreciated von Bidder's attention and discretion when I would impress a client with a table at the Four Seasons.

When the restaurant celebrated its milestone 50-year anniversary in 2009, about 1,200 customers showed up for the party. Keep in mind, the country was in a recession then. But unfortunately for its patrons, in 2019 after a year at a new location on 49th Street, the restaurant closed permanently.

During the Four Seasons' heyday, von Bidder became so well known for his operation of the restaurant that he was asked to teach courses on manners at New York University.

"First, evaluate the situation," von Bidder said he would advise students. "For example, if you're going to the boss's house for the first time, you need to fit in with every life situation." Know beforehand how formal the gathering is—you don't want to show up in shorts and sandals while everyone else is sporting khakis and a blazer. It's thoughtful to bring a small gift, such as premium chocolates; avoid cut flowers, pretty as they might be, which make your host pause from whatever they're doing to search for a vase.

"It's a different perspective in your house, when you're the host. But even then you have an obligation to be respectful of your guests, to know what they like or don't like, or maybe they are vegetarian."

Your obligation is to make everyone feel comfortable and pleased to be invited. Von Bidder quotes George Washington: "The taste of the roast depends on the greeting of the host." A meal with guests can be an unforgettable experience with a distinct purpose beyond nourishment.

Manners, such as promptness for dinner at the boss's house, carry over into understanding your role in business situations or particular events. Many law firms, for example, would host private parties at the Four Seasons with guest lists that included employees and clients.

"A lot of people in their 20s, 30s, know what to do at work, but not at cocktail parties," von Bidder told me. "Brilliant and nice-looking people would be sticking together instead of circulating." They should know they are there to mingle with clients, get to know their interests and make them feel valued to be involved with your firm or business.

I have seen this many times myself, for example, at charity events where a corporation would have a table and everyone would sit there talking with each other instead of taking the opportunity to network with others, whether they are from other businesses or are civic leaders.

At a place like the Four Seasons—or any restaurant—you will encounter all sorts of people and situations. I asked von Bidder how he responded respectfully to difficult customers.

"I always greeted each individual properly," he said. "You have to read people. You don't seat competitors next to each other. One time we had a bank executive who was accused of improper money transfers, and the attorney general who was prosecuting the case, arrive after the courtroom—both wanting to celebrate." Each, with their entourages, were discreetly shown to tables at opposite areas of the restaurant. That is respecting the customer, no matter their position—and not taking sides.

The times it was hard to show respect was when a customer was mean to the staff. Von Bidder considered it his job to protect his staff. He told me about the time a prince from a Middle Eastern country refused to be served his meal by a woman. Von Bidder declined to give him a different waiter. "'What do you mean?'" the prince said indignantly, "you're her boss and I'm your boss!"

Von Bidder had to stand up for his staff. He told the prince: "'I respect where you come from and you're a billionaire, but we're not playing by your rules.'" After a brief pause, he said, "I actually felt sorry for him."

You'd better believe that the restaurant staff recognized the respect shown to them by their boss in that situation. They must have felt valued.

Difficult people were rare, however. But tricky situations could arise at any time and von Bidder had to know how to be nimble and treat customers well. He likened it to putting on a Broadway show 30 times a week.

One day Jacqueline Kennedy Onassis came to the restaurant. (Incidentally, a party for 375 donors who paid $1,000 each was held at the Four Seasons for her husband President John F. Kennedy's 45th birthday in 1962, hours before a larger, and more famous, event at Madison Square Garden where Marilyn Monroe sang "Happy Birthday, Mr. President.") In the mid-1970s Jacqueline Kennedy Onassis became a book editor at nearby Doubleday and lived on Fifth Avenue. This day, her visit was unexpected; no table was available. Of course von Bidder would find a way to accommodate the former first lady. What to do? He couldn't kick out another guest midway through a meal to free a table, after all. He had to find a no-fuss solution that didn't embarrass Onassis.

"So we added a tiny square table by the window," von Bidder said. A hurried accommodation turned out to be a plus for the restaurant. "It became permanent. The Jackie O table." Everyone wanted to sit there because she did.

He recalled what it was like when the epitome of elegance entered a room of the restaurant. "Every conversation came to a standstill whenever she walked in. Jackie O modeled for me what respect was. With her soft voice she took delight in everything. Like she would say, 'This is the most delicious chocolate ever!' She was totally focused, made eye contact, paid attention. She accepted me as a person." That is the ultimate sign of respect.

We could all learn from her graciousness.

■ ■ ■

Alex von Bidder gave us some practical tips on acquiring good manners. Let's explore further. As the eighteenth-century Irish novelist Laurence Sterne wrote, "Respect for ourselves guides our morals, respect for others guides our manners."[2]

At their best, manners are an expression of respect for the other. In other words, respect is internal; manners are external. They are action.

Some might be in the category of social lubricant—such as greeting a hello. This is good, but can we change the script, please?

How many times has someone said to you, "Hi, how are you?" And then not bothered to hear your reply. How many times have you automatically responded, "Fine. How are you?" And you both walk away feeling a bit superficial.

Maybe you're not really fine, but passing an acquaintance in the grocery store is not the time to delve into your sore back or worries about your 401(k). But there is a way to respond authentically, without robotic platitudes.

For starters, greet someone by name; we all like to hear our own name. It's personal. Make eye contact. You might—or might not— offer your hand to shake. The COVID-19 pandemic upended this nicety and even now years later some remain hesitant; look for body language before you extend your hand. Of course, circumstances also dictate what's appropriate. The grocery store, for example, is casual where physical greetings are not necessarily expected. But in the office, a handshake, or even a quick fist bump, can be anticipated. Nothing more physical, though, such as a hug.

The overworn "How are you?" sounds meaningless. Come up with something more sincere, yet brief, such as "Good to see you, Jane; I hope you're well." That's warm and invites dialogue. I am not giving you a set of lines here. What you say must be authentic to *you*, whether you're asking the question or responding.

I can't resist telling you of one of the most memorable replies I've heard in response to my admittedly general, "How ya doing?"

"Still on the right side of the ground!" said the acquaintance, with eyes twinkling. We both laughed. I felt uplifted.

His response works because it was surprising and witty. The phrase might not work for you—it has to feel right for your personality—but you get the idea. Avoid meaningless autoreplies; be real.

Consider other ways that cliches enter your conversation and thereby dull the chance for meaningful connection. We heard von Bidder's advice to mingle at cocktail parties, especially if it's aimed at your company's clients. This is solid advice. But sometimes what we *should do* and what we *want to do* are contradictory. With that in mind, it might not surprise you to know that a majority of people dread small talk.

I have a friend, a writer, who calls small talk just filling air. It's of no consequence, he maintains, and is no more satisfying than an air-popped fake chip.

Small talk as a label has been around for a long time, though, centuries, in fact. The first use of the phrase is credited by the *Oxford English Dictionary* to Lord Chesterfield, an eighteenth-century British parliamentarian, in his book *Letters to His Son: On the Fine Art of Becoming a Man of the World and a Gentleman.*

"There is a sort of chit-chat, or smalltalk, which is the general run of conversation at courts, and in most mixed companies. It is a sort of middling conversation, neither silly nor edifying; but, however, very necessary for you to become master of," he wrote in a 1751 letter.

I wonder how his son reacted; probably not eager to learn how to have a "middling conversation."

Today, many Americans apparently would rather sit in silence than engage in small talk. A survey by the online language learning company Preply found that a whopping 71% of Americans prefer silence to small talk. Though the 2022 survey was a relatively small sampling—1,004 people—the finding is startling.

Many consider small talk awkward, and particularly dislike talking about sports or current events. Marriage isn't high on the list, either.

"Small talk might soon be a lost art," wrote Matt Zajechowski, in a 2024 blog update on the survey. "We learned that 2 in 3 Americans have used their phones to avoid making small talk."[3]

Apparently there's a generational difference. Among baby boomers, 30% were prone to check their phones instead of starting a conversation but with Gen Zers, the number nearly tripled to 89%.

When they do engage in small talk, half of those surveyed said they do so to be polite and avoid awkwardness. This occurs most often in retail stores, grocery stores, work, and home—in that order. The top three go-to topics when meeting someone for the first time are weather, plans, and work, not surprisingly as they generally are universal and inoffensive. Not a good idea to jump into national politics when first meeting someone!

Politeness isn't a bad motivator, in my opinion. But what is it about small talk that so many would rather avoid it, even to the point of rudeness?

The survey didn't probe the *why*. But it's fairly easy to come up with reasons, whether valid or not: small talk is superficial. It goes nowhere. It's banal. A waste of time. We feel judged to be not particularly interesting or witty. (Or maybe we're the ones judging.)

"Though it can certainly be awkward at times, small talk is still a persistent part of American culture. Idle chatter can bring us together and serves as a conversational starting point for people who might not know each other well—and even those that do," wrote Zajechowski.

Given that we can't completely avoid small talk—and maybe we shouldn't—it's worthwhile to know how to do it painlessly. A key to surviving, maybe even enjoying, extended small talk is to be prepared. By extended, I mean conversations that go further than a quick comment at the local coffee shop.

Be prepared with some topics, and then have some follow-up questions or comments in mind. Then let the small talk flow into more meaningful conversation.

If you are nervous about starting a conversation, then try these simple strategies before you begin:

- **Be positive.** Don't worry about how you will come across. Focus on the other person and what they are saying, and how they are saying it.
- **Take a deep breath.** Nothing helps lift nervousness like a good cleansing breath to the very bottom on your lungs. Relax your shoulders; don't fidget.
- **Keep expectations minimal.** If you expect the conversation will lead to a job offer, a new business contract, a lifelong friendship, then the pressure is on and disappointment could be the result. But if you anticipate that at least you made a human connection, then you can feel fulfilled.

Think of small talk as consisting of three parts: the icebreaker that gets the talk going, connection wherein questions lead to something in common or of interest, and then a graceful way to exit. Don't just look at your watch and walk away!

Introduce yourself and have an open-ended question ready, something that cannot be answered with a simple yes or no. Good topics for the icebreaker include food: "What do you recommend at that new restaurant downtown? I'm hoping to try it soon." "What's your favorite dinner to make during the week, I'm looking for new ideas?" Hometown is another fine topic: "Where did you grow up?" "What brought you to this town/city?"

Topics to avoid with strangers include finances, past relationships, appearance, and gossip. These are either too personal, judgmental, or tawdry.

What's in It for Me?

Connection happens depending on the answer to your icebreaker. Instead of rummaging through your mind for the next question, be at ease and listen to the other person. You just might discover something in common. Keep this part going until it feels forced or has run out of steam. Signs of boredom include the other person looking around the room while you're talking. Or maybe you're finding the impulse to do so.

A graceful exit leaves the other person feeling good; by all means avoid vacuous excuses. Say the person's name and thank them. "Jane, it's been a pleasure speaking with you; I hope to see you again before too long and hear how your learning French is going." (Or whatever was mentioned.)

Some people seem to have a knack for remembering names, but actually it's a skill that can developed. Here's how. When you are introduced, focus on the person and repeat their name out loud. Use their name in your conversation. Say it again when leaving. Memory experts advise to link the name to an image or another person, and while those strategies might work, I find the drill distracting. Generally, saying the name three times—repeating it when introduced, mentioning it in the conversation, including it in the farewell—is enough to embed in memory. But if not, the next time you meet and you just can't pull out the other's name, assume they can't, either. A brief—"Hi, I'm Bob,"—will likely lead to a response—"Hi, Pat here." And you both will be relieved!

Small talk builds a bridge between you and someone else. What you talk about doesn't matter as much as the fact that you're talking. With preparation, it can instill confidence. But avoiding small talk—looking at your phone or rejecting invitations to gatherings—can contribute to anxiety and isolation. Push yourself.

While it's handy to be prepared with questions to ask besides the ubiquitous "How are you?," take it to another level and lay the groundwork to truly connect with another person.

Here are some steps to try:

- **Build trust.** Share something about yourself to go further than social niceties. "When we take the first step and are willing to share more about how we are actually feeling and what's really on our minds, we allow the person we are speaking with to do the same," said Saba Harouni Lurie, a licensed marriage and family therapist, in a *VeryWellMind* article updated in 2024. "It's a way to signal that we want to have a more honest and in-depth conversation and can serve as an invitation for the other person to do the same."[4]
- **Actively listen.** Be fully present, undistracted, and paying attention to unspoken messages. This is the foundation for meaningful conversation in which all feel understood and valued.
- **Have genuine curiosity.** You're not just absorbing information; be curious about why or how the other person did what they are telling you about.
- **Be nonjudgmental.** Let the other person know you are supportive; they can trust you. Replace the urge to criticize with kindness.

The next time someone initiates small talk with you by commenting on the weather—even though it's obvious whether it is raining or windy or sunny—instead of thinking of it as banal, appreciate the effort. At least the other person didn't whip out their cell phone to avoid talking with you. Find some humor in the moment.

As Oscar Wilde, an Irish playwright known for his wit, wrote, "I love talking about nothing. It is the only thing I know anything about."[5]

■ ■ ■

Conveying respectfulness through your good manners extends beyond politeness. Let's say you are invited to a dinner party—maybe it's with your boss, maybe a group of loosely connected

What's in It for Me?

acquaintances. You take your cues from the host, make small talk, praise the potatoes. That's enough, right? Only if you don't want to be invited again.

You should be bringing something to the table, something more than a bottle of Cabernet. You must be prepared to advance the conversation, to take it in unexpected directions. Liven things up For example: "I've been reading an interesting book that makes a case, a nearly sacrilegious case, for someone else writing many of Shakespeare's plays and sonnets. A woman! What do you think? I mean, could one person actually write 38 plays and more than 150 sonnets in his lifetime of only 52 years?"

Or "The other night I was thinking about when I lost my first tooth; I don't know why. Even after the Tooth Fairy left a dime under my pillow, I still remember the shock that a part of my body fell out ... and wondered ... *what's next?*! Does anyone else remember how that felt?"

Or "I have a confession ... I have the urge to kill my sourdough starter. It's there on my kitchen counter every day waiting like my cat to be fed but no matter how much bread I make, some starter is still left ... and needs to be fed! It's alive and so I can't really kill a living thing but does this ever end?"

Okay, maybe the last two examples are silly, but depending on the crowd you'll get the table buzzing. People laughing. People sharing experiences. People who are glad you are there and will want to see you the next time.

This is part of your responsibility of being a guest, good manners and underneath it, unsaid but felt, a measure of respectfulness to the host. Knowing what is expected of you as a guest, a host, an employee in a social situation or other occasions relieves stress. You are prepared, in control. You appear confident.

Innumerable books have been written about manners and I am not going to duplicate them with advice you already know, such as sending a brief but detailed thank-you note.

■ ■ ■

But the societal construct of please-and-thank-you manners can become outdated. Then how do you act? Not that long ago, for example, it was customary for a man to hold a door open for a woman. He was considered respectful. Today? That once chivalrous act could be insulting! Women have the strength to open doors for themselves, of course.

Kelly McKenzie, the author and antique dealer, realized the shift in decorum. "While back in the day having someone do this for you was a mark of respect, today it's different. It can be viewed as condescending."

I have a friend who avoids the situation—and makes a point—by getting to the door before the guy and opening it for him. She said her husband has come to appreciate it.

It's important to consider the other person's social cues.

Are they striding toward the door with their head up and shoulders back? If so, they could feel disrespected if you rush to hold it open. They could view it as if you see them as being "less" or incapable, McKenzie said.

If you are the confident woman for whom the door is opened, how do you react?

Attitude is everything. "When someone grins at me or says 'hi' as they hold the door, I appreciate their effort to connect with me," McKenzie said. "I value the connection over the gesture."

Dr. Miguel Cardona, the former US Secretary of Education, said a level of emotional intelligence is helpful in navigating around tricky situations. "You have to read the social cues and to respond and adapt to them appropriately, while also staying true to your values," he said.

Allia Zobel Nolan, an internationally published author of more than 150 books including *Why a Cat Is Better Than a Man*, has some thoughts on the matter.[6] "I consider myself to be a capable woman and always have and I really wouldn't take offense at anyone holding the door open for me. I think something like this has taken on too much of this 'I can do it for myself' aura, when, in fact, whether it's a man or a woman, holding the door for someone is just a civil, nice thing to do," she said.

"Letting it close in someone's face, male or female, is just in my humble opinion, rude."

■ ■ ■

Life can be stressful when you're trying to read social cues or deal with unrespectful people. Alex von Bidder handled it this way: when you're in an uncomfortable situation, just breathe into it. As you might guess, he practices yoga—he's a certified instructor—and meditates.

Practicing yoga affects the mind in a good way, he said. "You learn a lot about yourself and you learn a lot about your mind." Be centered. It's good for you and influences the atmosphere in the room or place.

"If you are grounded and in the right frame of mind, you can endure anything. I'm not saying I wasn't ever nervous about sitting 200 people, but if I focused, those were just little distractions, not disasters," he said. Be the calm in the eye of the storm.

Deepak Sethi, a leadership development expert whose work has been featured in the *Wall Street Journal* and *USA Today* and is a frequent speaker at leadership conferences, said most of us take our minds for granted. Thankfully, that is a mistake which can be fixed.

"Despite all the talk about the mind-body connection and the recognition that the human mind is a supercomputer, most of us do not even scratch the surface in terms of using our mind to maintain our mental and physical health and to enhance and embellish our lives," he said in article titled "Total Self-Transformation Using Mindfulness" in the Spring 2024 issue of *Leader to Leader* online magazine.[7] "Practicing mindfulness meditation every day is the equivalent to physical exercise, in terms of keeping the mind calm and functioning at its very peak," he wrote.

We ought to live our life based on our values, but the problem is that generally we do not have much clarity on what they are or what it means to live by them. Sethi uses this following exercise which he has given to hundreds of executives. "I ask them to list their key values on a sheet of paper. I then tell them to turn over the page, not look at it, and on a second page list the key activities they spend their time on during the week," he said. Then they are asked to compare.

Often, this is eye-opening, or should we say, mind-opening. Time is our most precious resource and we often do not consider how we allocate it. Does the time you spend during the week align with your values? How can that be improved?

You might well ask what all this talk about manners, small talk, connections, and mindfulness has to do with our overall topic of respectfulness. The answer: they offer a glimpse into the elements that can lead to respectfulness into our everyday lives and a path to navigating forward. But there's much more to consider in coming chapters.

We began discussing what's in it for you—what are the benefits—to being respectful.

Over time, you will see many benefits to being respectful and acting accordingly. I mentioned three earlier: improved relationships, strengthened professional connections, and the easing of stress. You will find more.

I hope you will embrace respectfulness as a personal value, a cornerstone of your character, as it improves your life and those around you.

What's in it for you? Everything.

Think About It

1. How do you deal with disrespectful people? Do you get emotional and take it personally? What could be a better way?
2. Do your manners adequately and authentically express your sense of respectfulness?
3. The next time you greet a friend in passing, say something other than "How are you?" And note the reaction. Think of a new response when you are asked, "How are you?"

CHAPTER 4

Start with Self-Respect

Respect yourself and others will respect you.
— Confucius

Respectfulness begins with the way you respect yourself. You cannot be authentically respectful of others if you're not coming from a solid foundation within. Similarly, you won't attract sincere respect from others if you lack respect for yourself.

This sounds simple, but the more we examine self-respect the more complicated the quality actually is. Self-respect is not synonymous with self-esteem, though they are linked. It is not equivalent to having a healthy ego or even to liking yourself. Lacking self-respect can lead to servility, a sense of inferiority. Conversely, if overabundant, self-respect can veer into arrogance and a sense of superiority. You don't want either.

The expression of self-respect can range from taking care of yourself to adhering to strong moral convictions—and everything in between. One way to think about it: if you focus on respecting others without first respecting yourself, then you are untethered and vulnerable to the opinions and reactions of others toward you. You look for validation outside of yourself. This is not fulfilling; worse, it is never enough.

Even if you're saying about now, "Oh, I don't need this; I already respect myself," keep reading. It's time to dust off assumptions, see what's underneath, and rebuild or strengthen the core.

Self-respect is of great importance in everyday life. "It is regarded as both morally required and as essential to the ability to live a satisfying, meaningful, flourishing life," according to *The Stanford Encyclopedia of Philosophy*.[1]

You have significant worth, no matter your upbringing, culture, social status, education, financial accumulation, or whatever criteria are typically attributed to "worth."

The eighteenth-century German philosopher Immanuel Kant postulated that an individual has dignity and moral status just by virtue of being a rational human and therefore is entitled to self-respect. You can see how this belief is intertwined with his views on respect accorded others, as we discussed in Chapter 2.

You might agree that a person is entitled to self-respect but that does not necessarily guarantee that you feel it for yourself within the inner dark spaces we try to avoid, especially in the middle of the night when we cannot sleep.

The author Joan Didion wrote with insight about self-respect. "To have that sense of one's own intrinsic worth which constitutes self-respect is potentially to have everything: the ability to discriminate, to love, and to remain indifferent," she wrote in the essay "On Self-Respect," part of the *Slouching Towards Bethlehem* collection.[2] "To lack it is to be locked within oneself, paradoxically incapable of either love or indifference."

Without self-respect, Didion wrote, "one eventually discovers the final turn of the screw: one runs away to find oneself, and finds no one at home." Don't let that be you.

■ ■ ■

Michael J. Dowling grew up outside Knockaderry, a small village in County Limerick, Ireland. The family was impoverished, but as Dowling sees it, they were not poor.

"I grew up in an environment where, when you were poor, you were disrespected, you were treated very poorly," he said. "Your environment impacts you. But the decision you make regarding it is what defines you over time."

> *Michael Dowling was the president and CEO of Northwell Health in New York and Connecticut from 2002, leading it through tremendous growth before becoming CEO emeritus in 2025. Previously, he was a professor at Fordham University and director of its Tarrytown, New York, campus, then assistant dean at the Graduate School of Social Services. He also is a former instructor at the Harvard School of Public Health Center for Continuing Professional Education.*
>
> *In public service, he served as New York's director of Health, Education and Human Services and was deputy secretary to former governor Mario Cuomo. He also was the commissioner of New York's Department of Social Services.*
>
> *Among the books he has written,* Leading Through a Pandemic: The Inside Story of Humanity, Innovation, and Lessons Learned During the Covid-19 Crisis *details Northwell's response in the epicenter of the pandemic.*
>
> *Dowling's many awards include The Conference Board's 2023 Committee for Economic Development Distinguished Leadership Award, the 2021 Glassdoor Employees' Choice Award, the Columbia University School of Business 2020 Deming Cup for Operational Excellence, the Gail L. Warden Leadership Excellence Award from the National Center for Healthcare Leadership, the National Human Relations Award from the American Jewish Committee, the Ellis Island Medal of Honor and the Gold Medal from the American Irish Historical Society.*

Today Dowling is the CEO emeritus of Northwell Health, the largest health-care provider and private employer in New York state with a workforce of more than 105,000 and annual revenue of

$23 billion. Most recently, Northwell was approved to expand into western and southern Connecticut and join with the multi-hospital Nuvance Health.

Dowling had led the clinical, academic, and research enterprise since 2002 and through the uncharted challenge of the COVID-19 pandemic, which early on struck the New York City metro area particularly hard. To navigate a medical team's response through the long pandemic took fearless leadership.

I've known Dowling for many years, since he first came to the States. He's a terrific human being who cares about health care, and he cares about the patients at a very basic level. He cares about the nurses and assistants and those who work alongside them to make sure something comes out positively. He's a 24/7 guy.

He has never asked anybody for something he wouldn't do himself.

Your career is one way to define you; character attributes are another. Dowling defines himself as an optimist. And talking with him or hearing one of his lectures, his optimism toward life is evident. And yet considering his childhood, it's unexpected.

Dowling was one of five siblings. Their father's work as a laborer was halted by rheumatoid arthritis; their mother was totally deaf since the age of seven. Financially, the family struggled.

"You know, poverty is a wonderful builder of resilience in many ways," Dowling told me recently with his typical optimistic outlook. "Rather than looking at a difficult experience as a negative, and always whining about how bad it is and because of it you're now a victim—I don't buy into that argument at all. What that did in my situation is that it allowed me to build up a lot of self-respect for myself and my family.

"But I wasn't going to take crap from anybody."

He credits his mother with instilling a sense of self-worth in her children. "She wanted us as kids to understand that we were worth something, that our future was not going to be determined by the environment we were in. She would say things like, 'Never allow your current circumstances to limit your future potential.'

Start with Self-Respect

"We were poor but never let it restrict our potential; because of my mother's attitude we always looked forward and believed in the power of education."

Dowling admits now that "for a number of years I had a little bit of a chip on my shoulder because of the way you were treated when you're poor like this," but he was determined eventually to deal with his environment in a positive way. He took responsibility for his life. He put on his boots and pulled himself up by the bootstraps. From that small village in Ireland, he went on to earn degrees at University College Cork and Fordham University, have important positions in areas as varied as academia and state government, and become a leader and influential voice in health care.

He knows people from all over the world. He never turned his back on Ireland, however. Dowling is proud of his Irish heritage.

How do you begin to turn around your outlook?

Look in the mirror, he said. "Ask yourself, 'What do you think of the person looking back at you in the mirror?' You like the guy; you respect the guy? Or you hate the son of a bitch. Right?

"How do you feel about yourself? And then you build it, build that sense of confidence."

A step toward building is to do something, make it something that speaks to you and tugs at you, even if lightly at first. Maybe it's learning to play the guitar or to speak another language, maybe it's volunteering to read a book or teach a craft to children at your local library's story hour. Succeed at that something, whatever it is.

"That helps you convince yourself that you have a capability that you didn't think you had," Dowling said. You won't get that reinforcement sitting on the couch—you've got to act. "Take some risk or do something."

■ ■ ■

Once you've felt the uplift from accomplishing something you hadn't realized was within your ability, stretch further and summon up a dose of courage. Push yourself beyond your safe zone and do something that scares you a little bit. It doesn't mean you have to swim with sharks or take up stock car racing. Just something that pushes you to another level.

Former Senator Phil Gramm took a leap not many would do: he ran for president of the United States. This is not for the faint of heart! Gramm was seeking the Republican Party nomination for the 1996 presidential race. By mid-1994 he had already raised $8 million for the campaign, more than any other GOP candidate at the time. But, as politics goes, he came in second in the Louisiana caucuses and six weeks later was the fifth-highest vote getter in the pivotal Iowa caucuses. Shortly after that disappointing showing, Gramm withdrew. Bob Dole was number one in Iowa and went on to win the party's nomination but lost the race to Democratic President Bill Clinton who was going for a second term.

Gramm told me he has no regrets for taking the risk he did. "My view of the campaign was I was the wrong person at the wrong time, but when the time comes you either had to do it or not do it and I didn't want to be sitting on the front porch in a rocking chair someday and saying, 'I wonder if?' So I have no bitter memories about it. I met a lot of people and my opinion of the country went up during the campaign."

The front-porch-rocking-chair is a good litmus test for a challenging situation.

"There's an old country song that has lyrics like: 'I'll never know 'til it's over if I'm right or I'm wrong loving you. But I'd rather be sorry for something I've done than something I didn't do.'

"And that's the way I feel about life," Gramm said. "I'd rather make an error doing something than not doing it." You will see more of Gramm's views on politics and American life today in Chapter 8.

People with character tend to have self-respect, David Brooks said in his book *The Road to Character*.[3] It is not dependent on IQ or other gifts you were fortunate to receive at birth.

"It is not earned by being better than other people at something," Brooks wrote. "It is earned by being better than you used to be."

Reread that sentence. He is talking about meeting challenges, reaching for continual growth.

"Self-respect is produced by inner triumphs, not external ones," he wrote.

Keep pushing, no matter how "old" you may get. In fact, continuing to push yourself as the years go by is crucial to maintaining self-respect and quality of life. Wake up each morning excited for what the day may bring—what you may make happen.

You can hear the yogi in Alex von Bidder's admonition in an interview called "Being Deep, Light, and Mindful" for the Ageist podcast in 2021.[4] He actually was the first guest of the podcast and his story was so fascinating that they reran it. You will remember von Bidder, the former manager and partner of the storied Four Seasons restaurant in Manhattan from Chapter 3.

"Most people, as they get older, whatever scares them, they try to avoid," von Bidder said.[5] "And when you do that your life shrinks."

■ ■ ■

While taking meaningful action, also give yourself the space for introspection. Identify your values, why they are important to you, how they fit into your life—or, if they don't, how you can make them do so.

Though not everyone will have the same ones, of course; some values might be integrity, generosity, kindness, loyalty, and spirituality. Think of people you admire and why.

Keep your list of values to a manageable size to work with initially. As you think about it, you'll see how things relate. For example, if ethical personal conduct in your workplace is valued, that translates to integrity. Do what you say you're going to do. Build trust.

I would like to share with you a story of how I learned at an early age about integrity. The lesson was from my father, S. J. Dilenschneider, who led by example.

Dad ran the *Columbus Citizen*, a leading community newspaper in Columbus, Ohio. One day, a prominent businessman died by suicide. Should the newspaper publish the story? He had been a public figure.

Dad said, "Run it."

Before long, his phone rang and I eavesdropped on the call. "You run that story and we're taking all of our advertising out of the newspaper!" bellowed the man on the other end of the line. He was an executive of a large department store in the city where the businessman had worked. Naturally, the store's ties to the community ran deep. But so did the newspaper's. The editor had to be fair; no favors when it came to what went in the news or stayed out of it. Threats wouldn't work.

My father was steadfast; a short story about the suicide was published. As promised, the department store pulled all of its advertising. I don't recall the percentage, but it was a huge blow to the paper's income.

About 10 days later there was a knock at my father's office door. In walked Fred Lazarus Jr., who owned a competing department store. "We're going to double our commitment," he told my father, "and drive the other guy out of business!" And that's exactly what he did.

F&R Lazarus & Company, founded in 1851, later became Federated Department Stores and in 2007 was renamed Macy's Inc. for the chain it had acquired the previous decade. Today, it is the leading retail department store enterprise, by retail sales, in the world.

My father stood up for what he believed in; he was guided by the ethics of his profession and could not be swayed by financial considerations. Fortunately, it worked out well. But either way, my father would have maintained his integrity and self-respect.

Do your day-to-day actions align with what you value or is there a disconnect? Perhaps you have felt this disconnect but could not identify the source. Actions and values must be in harmony for a life of authenticity.

Is there any area you are not willing to compromise about? Where do you draw the line?

■ ■ ■

Start with Self-Respect

Do you draw a line when the question is your time? If you are putting yourself last for your own attention, you are not necessarily helping the others you put first. You might see yourself as altruistic, but eventually feel like a martyr or at least out of sync. You are ignoring the "self"; you are not respecting yourself and your time.

We all have obligations that affect our time; we must accommodate family life, especially if we have young children. But you can look for pockets of time to feed your "self." Could you get up 15 minutes earlier to meditate in quiet or to sip coffee while reading the news before the rest of the household awakes? How about 20 minutes to go outside for a walk or run? How about even five minutes to look out the window and observe the slant of the sun or the cover of clouds? Think of what grounds you, then honor your "self" with respect for your time.

S. P. Hinduja became one of the world's wealthiest people through various enterprises such as banking. Yet while he was building his family's enterprise, first from their native India, then London, Switzerland, and New York City, he always made time for meditation. Every day he would rise before 5 a.m., meditate, then go for a brisk walk, tending to the spiritual and physical aspects of self. As he walked, he often dispensed seed to birds and peanuts to squirrels along the way.

I knew and admired S. P.; a chapter in my book on *Character*[6] is devoted to him. Some months after he died in 2023 at the age of 87, his family shared with me his written reflections. "Why do routine and discipline matter?" he wrote. "The answer is that with both serving as your foundation, you can actually get things done!"

Self-care could be physical, such as putting effort into eating fresh, unprocessed food, as S. P. did. Or, if you don't have time for daily walks while feeding the wildlife, then look for ways to exercise in spurts, such as taking the stairs instead of the elevator or not always pulling into the closest parking spot.

Self-care extends to social and emotional needs. Consider the people you choose to have close in your life. Are they generally supportive and build you up or do they knock you down? Is the relationship all about the emotional energy you can give them? If you allow a one-sided relationship, even within a family, then you are eroding self-respect. Time for an honest conversation. Keep it unemotional.

Surround yourself, in widening ripples, with people who empower.

■ ■ ■

Coming from a place of self-respect enables a generosity of spirit. Aretha Franklin's song "Respect" became an anthem. *Rolling Stone* magazine named it the greatest song of all time in 2021 and again in its 2024 revision.[7] That designation may be debated, but there's no doubt the call for respect went from a request to a demand in the national psyche.

Aretha was only 24 when she recorded the song, yet she had "the poise, authority and confidence of someone who had been singing for 60 years. Her voice was young and vital but it also came from a place of ancient secret wisdom," wrote David Ritz in his book *From These Roots*.[8] "Respect" put Aretha into orbit, is how he put it.

But did you know that Otis Redding recorded the song first? He wrote it, in fact! His version reached the top five on Billboard's Black Singles Chart in 1965 and number 35 on pop charts. It was a success for him. Two years later, Aretha belted it out and pressed it into vinyl.

When Redding first heard Aretha Franklin's version, he smiled. "The girl has taken that song from me. Ain't no longer my song," he said. "From now on, it belongs to her."[9]

Redding showed respect for Aretha making her mark with "Respect" and in so doing reflected self-respect. He wrote the song; he made it a hit—that was enough, no resentment. Now it was hers.

■ ■ ■

We've talked about building self-respect, living it, and letting it show. But you also have to be aware of the threats to it. That might sound ominous, but what I mean is that you can build a nice fortress of self-respect but there are outside forces that can erode it.

To be blunt, you won't find lasting confidence through your electronic screen. We've talked much of the philosopher Immanuel Kant and his interpretation of respect and self-respect. But from the eighteenth century, there's no way he could have foreseen the social media phenomenon of today and how it permeates daily life, especially of the Gen Z age group (born 1997–2012) and, to an extent, the later edge of Millennials (born 1981–1996).

Michael Dowling sees social media from a health perspective and is alarmed. "Social media these days is a powerful source of negativity, which leads by the way, to an extraordinary increase in anxiety, depression, and suicide among the young," he told me. "I think that social media has benefits, but it has that disastrous side to it. In many ways it's a modem of communication for cowards who don't want to put their name on anything, but just put out its garbage out there and then get other people to follow it."

A danger with platforms such as TikTok and Instagram is that they encourage viewers to engage in comparison with others and be overly affected by the influencers. They compel followers to buy certain fashion because it is in, only two or three months later to have some other trends wash over it. Their motive? Profit. One day you've got to have a certain water bottle because the cool people do (on TikTok) and the next week it's a different brand. The influencers chase the consumers; the consumers chase the brand to be "in" like the influencers.

Self-respect? Hardly. It is self-comparison, which ends up making one feel inadequate. As Steve Jobs said, "Your time is limited. Don't waste it living someone else's life."

I am not saying that all social media is negative. At its best, it can link communities—whether geographically or by interest—and provide a means of rapid communication. But you have to be aware of its purpose. Come from a strong sense of self-respect so you are not buffeted around by the latest hot trend. An hour later there will be another.

More than so-called influencers, though, a downside of social media today is the aspect on some sites of anonymity. Anyone can say anything, and then others jump on it feeling validated. This is prevalent in politics today. And it creates an unhealthy stew of resentment and anger.

Former Senator Phil Gramm of Texas has a theory. "People who are disrespectful of others, I think in many cases don't respect themselves very much," he said. "The respect you show to other people to some degree reflects the respect you have for yourself."

The world would be a better place if people went out of their way to be respectful of others, he added.

Think about it—he is saying that people who are disrespectful are signaling a lack of self-respect. That is a whole other way to look at it. Perhaps that helps you understand others; perhaps yourself.

■ ■ ■

We've talked about self-respect being internal. Only you are responsible for it. Only you can tend it with the care you would give a rare orchid; only you can strengthen it.

One negative habit is to base your sense of self-respect on how you compare to others. Chances are you don't do this intentionally. This happens when a friend, coworker, maybe even a sibling appear to be smarter, better-looking, more popular, luckier—you name it—than you. Face it, life isn't fair.

Mel Robbins, a motivational speaker whose podcast surpassed 200 million downloads in 2025,[10] noted that the problem isn't the tendency to compare. "The problem is what you're doing with the comparison that matters," she said in her book *Let Them*.[11] "So ask yourself: What are you doing when you compare? Are you torturing yourself, or is it teaching you something important?"

Torture or teacher. Torture comes when you compare yourself to a fixed aspect of someone else's life that you cannot magically make appear in your own, for example, their height. "It is useless for your growth and detrimental to your happiness," Robbins said.

Psychologists call this upward comparison, which means measuring yourself against someone else who you think is better than you. If you can think dispassionately about it, you can see how destructive it is to your self-esteem. A downward comparison is thinking you are better in some way than others, which is damaging not only to them but also to yourself.

"If you're not careful, comparison can become the reason why you doubt yourself, procrastinate, and continue to stay stuck," Robbins wrote.

Instead, what can you learn from someone else's success, which was the result of something they could control? See the possibilities. Come up with a plan for what you can control for yourself.

■ ■ ■

Let's say you have a firm sense of your worth. Maybe your childhood was difficult—there are so many ways for that to happen, from trauma to deprivation to bullying—but like Michael Dowling you have tapped into strength.

You have credentials, have risen in your profession. But then some, no matter their achievements, feel like they don't deserve it. They feel like imposters. Could that be you?

You might feel like you know yourself, possess self-confidence, have self-respect. So where is that insecurity coming from: inside or from the way others have treated you? A disrespect, at work for example, can become internalized and by continually focusing on it you begin to think the disrespect is based on something true—that you are an imposter. I have seen this happen even to competent managers with multiple degrees.

Indra Nooyi understands. She has seen it among some women, and men, in the companies that she has led, such as the multinational giant PepsiCo.

"Very often people have self-respect, but then what happens is when they're treated disrespectfully," she told me. "They lose respect for themselves because then they start to question 'Maybe

I'm not competent. Maybe I don't deserve respect because I'm not competent.'"

"The minute you take away confidence, it is impacted because of this whole notion 'Am I good enough? Maybe I'm not good enough and that's why I'm treated badly.'"

If this is happening in the workplace, supervisors need to be aware and step in and restore a level of mutual respect.

"The problem is we can't afford to treat people badly; we just cannot. Because when you treat people badly they self-question and then lose confidence in themselves. That's the first loose brick in your life," Nooyi said. "Definitely it's more difficult for women than men, but it's getting better." You will read more about handling situations such as this in the workplace in Chapter 6.

Self-respect also involves standing up for yourself. This can be difficult for people who are uncomfortable with conflict; they avoid it at all costs—to themselves. But you don't have to be aggressive to be assertive. Speak calmly, without placing blame as that is sure to make the other person defensive.

I'm not saying that you should always assume you're right—see how tricky this gets? An inflated sense of worth breeds arrogance and eventually loneliness. No one can achieve perfection and few are the best at everything. No one never makes a misstep or two. Own them. Learn from them. But don't beat yourself up about them. Perhaps you've heard it said that even the top baseball players hit the ball on average only 3 times out of 10 at bat.

People who can let down the mask of perfection and allow a glimpse of vulnerability generally are respected. Why is that? Because others can see themselves falling short of perfection, too. It's a relief when someone admits it.

But this is hard to do. Today's culture, fueled by social media, showers attention on those who sound wittier, look thinner, appear more successful—the superlatives go on. As we have noted, the impulse is to compare ourselves to what is projected in social media feeds whether it's to a friend who looks to be having a fabulous vacation in a photo posted online or to an influencer who appears to have the epitome of a "with-it" life. The resulting envy or despair ultimately is harmful to any sense of self-respect.

A better tactic than measuring yourself against others—or your own impossible idea of perfection—is to ease up on yourself. Don't hide your true nature behind a protective facade of success or superior smarts or whatever. Allow at least friends and those close in your life to see the real you, imperfections and all. It's a gift, actually, because then they feel permission to do the same, to cast aside pretensions and be real. It feels good.

Now, I realize it can sound contradictory to say continually push yourself to improve and grow while simultaneously accepting missteps and flaws. But it is possible to hold both ideas and feel the roots of self-respect stretch deeper.

Sometimes people who appear successful actually have fierce inner critics. You know, that tendency to review your day in the middle of the night when a voice only you can hear nags, "Why didn't you do this? How could you have said that?" Some contemplation is fine, though I do recommend you don't do it at 3 a.m. But too much of an inner critic leads to feeling defeated, that maybe you're not up to the job or task or role. Instead, give yourself an inner cheerleader, a voice that will encourage you and acknowledge the good. Be kind to yourself as you would be to your best friend.

Like watering your plants with fertilizer once a month, feed your self-respect regularly. One way is to think of the people whom you respect and figure out why.

"It comes down to people who work hard, and through that hard work achieve something," author Allia Zobel Nolan told me, describing those she respects. "People who stand up for what they believe. People who overcome struggles and manage to keep their humor and humanity."

■ ■ ■

Mahatma Gandhi said, "I cannot conceive of a greater loss than the loss of one's self-respect."[12] I would add to that, one's reputation.

Reputation and self-respect are linked, of course. Like it or not, in certain parts of the world that are fighting other parts, reputation is critical. What is the reputation of the ruler of Russia?

Reputation can't be taken at face value. It doesn't last forever but you should know how it is formed. In your life, recognize what qualities to embrace for the reputation you want. Constructively nurture it; reputation is something to be prized. But as you rise professionally, it can also make you a target. A crisis—even if it's not your own doing—can destroy a fine reputation in no time. Be prepared for how you will handle the unexpected. This gets back to self-respect without going overboard into arrogance in which you fail to listen to others.

Reputation goes a lot further than "Here I am." It has everything to do with what you say and do and how you do it. When you have a good reputation, people want you to rub off on them. The downside is, once you lose your reputation, it's awfully hard to restore it.

With the sense of self-respect we've talked about, you can buttress your good reputation and weather a crisis, whether business or personal, that might come your way.

Acknowledge that you have intrinsic worth. Build your self-esteem by accomplishing something; take action. Then challenge yourself further.

Identify your values, such as integrity, honesty, and compassion, and make sure they align with your actions. Your anchor of self-respect will hold stronger.

Practice self-care; you ought not to lose yourself trying to please others. Avoid measuring your worth by comparing your life to others, a tendency encouraged by social media. That will eventually erode your self-respect. Guard your reputation.

We've covered a lot of ground in this chapter as we explored how to gain and maintain self-respect. You might want to reread some sections. A healthy sense of self-respect is essential to being able to authentically treat someone else with respectfulness.

Can you actually do all this?

Tennis legend Venus Williams knows: "Just believe in yourself. Even if you don't, pretend that you do, and at some point, you will."[13]

Think About It

1. Do you like the person you see in the mirror?
2. Identify your core values. Do they fit with your actions?
3. Do you look to others for validation? Think about how you can give yourself an inner cheerleader.

CHAPTER 5

The Top Five Qualities of Respectfulness

I never learned anything while I was talking. You cannot talk to people successfully if they think you are not interested in what they have to say or you have no respect for them.
– Larry King

Respectfulness is more than being polite. It is more than using good manners, though manners are an outward expression of respect and they can smooth social interactions. Respectfulness includes treating people as individuals, each with inherent dignity.

An atmosphere of respect—whether in the workplace, the family and personal relationships, or civic institutions—builds a sense of trust and well-being. We all need this to thrive, adults and children alike.

Although respectfulness does not fit snugly into one definition, we know what it is when we see it, when we feel it, when we are given it. The same is true for the opposite—when we are disrespected. Oh, we know that one right away.

MaryLou Pagano, the executive director of The Sheen Center for Thought and Culture in Manhattan, interacts with a variety of creative performers as well as patrons and staff every day. Naturally, all have different expectations and needs; all must be treated respectfully.

The Sheen Center for artistic expression and intellectual engagement encompasses a 273-seat theater, an 80-seat Black Box theater, an art gallery, rehearsal studios, and reception spaces. It is affiliated with the Catholic church, a place "Where art and spirituality meet."[1]

Hundreds of artists have performed at the center over the years, such as Kristin Chenoweth, Nora Jones, James Taylor, and Bernie Williams. (Full disclosure: I have been a guest speaker about leadership in America and my books at the Sheen Center.)

> *MaryLou Pagano was raised in Crestwood, a small hamlet in the city of Yonkers, New York. The youngest of three, she attended Catholic schools and graduated from Trinity College in Washington, DC, with a double major in sociology and business management.*
>
> *She began her career in the development office of The Archdiocese of New York and has remained in development and fundraising for her almost 40-year career working in various Catholic institutions throughout New York, including Elizabeth Seton Children's, Iona Preparatory School, and the Church of St. Raymond's.*
>
> *She is the executive director of The Sheen Center for Thought and Culture, the performing arts center of the Archdiocese of New York.*
>
> *MaryLou considers her most important development role was raising her three children with her husband, Ed. She has also done consulting work for various schools and served on the board of Mt. St. Michael's School in the Bronx. She enjoys traveling with her family.*

The Sheen Center's vision is to "provide a platform for provocative conversations about diverse and inclusive aspects of humanity as seen through the creative lens of faith and respect."[2] Note the word *respect*.

I have known MaryLou since about 2010. There was a moment when she was asked to take over the leadership of The Sheen Center and the truth is she was more than capable. She has really put the center on the map.

"Whether a patron or performer, I want everyone to have the same exact outstanding experience, to leave here feeling better than when it started," Pagano said, "and respectfulness is number one to achieving that goal."

As we study this chapter and read about the top five qualities of respectfulness, you'll hear more from Pagano, including how she dealt with a diva who misbehaved and required a scolding.

I have put together this list of the top five qualities of respectfulness as a useful tool to remember them. You might rank the qualities differently or include others. Make it your own. The list certainly could be more than five and we will touch on some others later in this chapter.

With each of these top five we will explore methods and tips to put them into practice:

5. Listen to others—really listen—instead of thinking about what you'll say next.
4. Understand that everyone has their own experiences and beliefs.
3. Be courteous; help others see the good.
2. Practice compassion; foster a sense of belonging.
1. Acknowledge the dignity of human life, no matter one's station, culture, or preferences.

Listen to Others—Really Listen—Instead of Thinking About What You'll Say Next

We've all had this happen: you'll be talking away about something important to you in the moment, and the other person responds with a distracted "yeah," maybe not even looking up. Worse than feeling unheard, we feel disrespected. That what we're saying doesn't matter, that *we* don't matter.

This scenario has played out in the workplace, in the home, even when dining out. Nowhere is it appropriate.

If you are that distracted listener—and let's admit it, we all have been at one time or another—the first imperative is to put down your cell phone. Extract yourself from your phone—at least for a short while! Put it face-down on a table, put it in your pocket or purse. Turn it off so you are not tempted to reach for it when a buzz, swoosh, or ring sounds. A boss would do well to visibly open a desk drawer and put the cell in there when an employee comes into the office for a meeting. Show respect by giving your employee, coworker, spouse, or friend full attention. You would want the same.

In this section, you will read a lot about listening because it is foundational. You cannot fulfill the other top items if you do not first understand the skills of being a good listener—and use them.

Most people would consider themselves good listeners, much the same way they think they're good drivers. Others might not think so! Many think listening amounts to three things: don't interrupt when someone else is speaking, signal you're listening with the occasional "mmm-hmm," and be able to repeat back what was said. "So what you're saying is ... ." Possibly you've heard this advice in management workshops.

But good listening is much more. If we don't listen well, we will not grow or learn or interact with others in a way that is rewarding to everyone. Not to listen well is to be selfish because we shut ourselves off from others.[3]

Sometimes you may be just too tired or worried or about to head into a meeting to be a good listener right then. If so, try to set another time for the conversation instead of rushing or going about it half-heartedly.

Too often we listen, but don't hear.

How many times have we engaged in a dispute and, instead of listening to what was being said, we were too busy thinking about the arguments we wanted to make? And how many times have we failed to listen because we were just too busy talking?

The Top Five Qualities of Respectfulness

Actively listen. You may have heard this term, which was coined by psychologist Carl Rogers in the 1950s. It means more than turning away from your phone, though that is a necessary first step. Actively listening is a communication skill. It goes beyond simply hearing what another person is saying; it seeks to understand the meaning and intent behind the words. It requires you to be focused and mindful.

Staying focused can be a challenge because we take in spoken words slower than we think. No wonder our thoughts tend to race ahead when someone else is talking to us. It's natural, the way our brains are wired.

To be fully present requires turning off your internal dialogue—How long will this conversation go on? How can I resolve the problem?—and tuning in to what the other person is saying.

Give the speaker your undivided attention. Show that you are listening. As mentioned, turn off or better yet put away your connection to the outside world via your cell and place your focus on who is speaking to you.

Be attuned to nonverbal signals. You know, shoulders high and tense, excessive throat clearing, or barely concealed anger in the clenched jaw. Is someone talking, unusually for them, fast out of nervousness or slowly to find the right words? Fidgeting? Perspiring?

Equally important, be aware of what nonverbal signals *you* are sending. Avoid folding your arms in front of yourself, which creates a physical do-not-enter barrier. Instead keep an open posture, what feels right and comfortable to you. Lean in, not back, in your chair.

In the days of top-down management, I've seen a manager handle a one-on-one with an employee in the office with hands clasped behind the head, elbows out, and feet crossed on top of the desk. An intimidating posture, right? Maybe even a caricature these days. But not a signal of someone who is ready to listen to another point of view. (And if you are a manger, then you absolutely need to hear other views.)

Be aware of your facial expressions. Are you frowning seemingly in judgment? Are you grinning out of sync with the seriousness of what is spoken?

Make eye contact to show you are present, listening, and want to hear what the other person wants to say. Sounds simple enough, but when do you break away from looking someone directly in the eyes? One of the mistakes in eye contact is staring. How much eye contact is weirdly too much? How much not enough? Each situation might be different, but in general rely on the 50/70 guide.[4] Maintain eye contact half the time while speaking and 70% of the time while listening. Hold contact for four or five seconds before glancing to the side. Look away slowly; darting eyes look nervous or shy. Avoid looking down—whether when speaking or listening—which signals that you lack confidence.

"Look them in the eye," advises former PepsiCo president and CEO Indra Nooyi. "Engage with them in a way that you'd like to be engaged. And it doesn't matter who these people are. You don't have to be a CEO or a leader. It can be any human being. Respectfulness should be a core tenet of society."

Communication happens with your eyes when you actively listen. Maintaining appropriate eye contact shows interest and presence. The speaker has your full attention.

When someone comes to you with a problem or gripe, it's tempting to step in and try to solve it. Resist that urge. Respect the speaker's ability to arrive at a solution. Avoid making snap judgments that shut off communication.

Instead, ask open-ended questions to discover more, such as "How did you feel?," "Why do you think that happened in that way?," or "Can you tell me more?"

Your questions should encourage them to talk, explain, give examples. Your questions should not influence what the other person has to say. "Did you really think that was going to end well when you slammed the door?" is an abrupt conversation stopper.

You have seen the advice to parrot back what the speaker has said. But the best listeners are more than sponges, merely absorbing everything they hear.

Leadership consultants Jack Zenger and Joseph Folkman analyzed coaching skills of 3,492 managers to identify the most effective listeners. Their findings, published in a *Harvard Business Review* article, "What Great Listeners Actually Do," surprised them.[5]

"Good listening is much more than being silent while the other person talks," they wrote. "To the contrary, people perceive the best listeners to be those who periodically ask questions that promote discovery and insight." Good listening was seen as a two-way dialogue.

The best listeners made the other person feel supported and created an environment where issues and differences could be discussed openly and honestly. Poor listeners were seen as competitive and using their silence to prepare a response. Instead, it should be a conversation with feedback in both directions with no one becoming defensive. Let's face it, though, self-discipline is required to push aside your emotions and reactions to what you are hearing.

Avoid passing judgment. A person who is speaking from the heart, whether about an intellectual or emotional issue, wants to be heard. They do not want to encounter a torrent of admonitions or second-guessing. Be open-minded, be empathetic.

Be patient. Sometimes, people who are talking cannot approach what they really want to say in a direct way, especially if it's something emotional. It may be a frustrating experience, but the relaxed attentive listener who patiently waits for the point or is even gently encouraging, may be the one who truly hears the message. The speaker will be grateful and happy that their words were heard and understood.

Often, those who are speaking do not want you to have all the answers or provide a blueprint for their lives. Sometimes, just the experience of sharing a problem or a feeling is all that is needed to create joy or serenity or even the energy and will to get on with the day.

Award-winning author Kelly McKenzie learned from her father, who was a good listener. "I appreciated his ability to soak up a conversation without interrupting. It's become important to me to actively listen to someone, for how else can I understand and appreciate what they're saying if I'm thinking how I can top their story?"

Active listening is an important communication and social skill applicable anywhere—the workplace, home, political gatherings—and with anyone—colleagues, spouses, children, other family members, and friends. It is a skill that can be learned and honed with practice.

Active listening shows respect. And that is rewarding for all.

Understand That Everyone Has Their Own Experiences and Beliefs

At first glance, this key to respectfulness would seem a no-brainer. Of course everyone has their own experience and beliefs. We are not cookie-cutter versions of each other, and that's okay.

But even a casual look into many social media sites proves otherwise. Vicious name-calling! Lambasting ideas! Crude put-downs! And they gain traction when reposted and clicks soar into the thousands and millions. Soon the impression is that a majority agrees and anyone who doesn't is out of it. Or worse.

You can have your own belief—as long as it's the same as mine, is the mantra. As the protest song from the 1960s goes, "Nobody's right if everybody's wrong."[6]

Historically, countries have seen waves of disrespect, even fear, of the "other." Internment camps were built in the United States during World War II to remove Japanese American citizens from their homes after the bombing of Pearl Harbor. In the mid- to late-nineteenth century, signs in shops blatantly stated "Irish Need Not Apply" as anti-immigration stances proliferated. Only a generation ago, Blacks and Jews—and before them Italians—were prohibited from joining some country clubs. Augusta National Golf Club in Georgia didn't admit female members until 2012.

The wave of intolerance in the United States now is not a new, singular phenomenon. But it is indicative of culture that has fallen into the morass of disrespect. As *New York Times* columnist and bestselling author David Brooks wrote in a column, paraphrasing Thomas Paine, "These are the times that try people's souls, and we'll see what we are made of."[7]

I believe that we are made of much more good than is indicative of what we read on social media sites. And, gratefully, I am not alone. Dr. Miguel Cardona, the former US education secretary, has dealt with people of many different cultures and perspectives over the course of his career. "You just have to recognize that everyone has their perspective. And they might not agree with you and you might not agree with them, but it doesn't mean that they're any less or that they don't deserve to be treated with respect.

"So that principle of respecting people or treating people the way you want to be treated doesn't go away because you ideologically are different than me." (You can read about Cardona's views on teaching respectfulness in the schools in Chapter 8.)

In other words, take the understanding that everyone has their own experiences and beliefs and go one step further into accepting people with experiences and beliefs different than yours in a respectful manner.

Rabbi Arthur Schneier, a thought leader based in New York City who has traveled around the world, advises that a way to bridge the gap of elemental differences is by listening respectfully. He puts words into action with his efforts to advance human rights and freedom in multiple countries through the foundation he established, Appeal of Conscience.

"I'll never forget meeting with Fidel Castro from 10:30 'til 2:30 in the morning. Solo, nonstop he talked. It was an interfaith delegation, with two priests, an Armenian bishop, a minister, and me," Schneier told me. "I did not interrupt him; I just let him talk and talk and talk. And when he finished, then I made my requests of aiding some religious communities in Cuba.

"Particularly when you're dealing with an adversary, if you really want to establish rapport, the dialogue must be respectful, even when you disagree."

You will read more about Rabbi Schneier's experiences, world view, and advice in Chapter 9. Another level of understanding and accepting is engaging, as the Rabbi did.

It takes the generosity of an open mind to engage—respectfully—with someone whose beliefs are counter to your own. It also requires a relinquishing of defensiveness.

"A very overused word is *tolerance*. But it has a nuance when it comes to respectfulness," said MaryLou Pagano of The Sheen Center. "We live in this world where my opinion matters more. That's ridiculous.

"For the world we're in right now, we need less opinion, less vocal and more listening."

Be Courteous; Help Others See the Good

Author Kelly McKenzie's mom, Frankie Robinson, when she was well into her 90s and beyond had a way of making younger people appreciate the worth of those of her advanced age. She didn't do it by lecturing.

"Whether it was impulsive or a duty, I believe respect breeds respect," McKenzie said. "When my mother was in her mid-90s she lived in an assisted living facility. Whenever a resident fell, the staff had to call the fire department; no one was allowed to pick anyone up. Mom respected this rule and would wait patiently for the firefighters.

"A talented artist, once she was back on her feet, she would always thank them by offering to show them something 'to lift their spirits.' After viewing her artwork, they would leave with a new respect for the abilities of the aged."

Too often older people can feel unseen by younger ones who overlook their ability to continue contributing positively to society. Frankie Robinson's approach is a way of showing instead of telling.

At times it might not take much effort really to be courteous and help others see the good in each other. A friend who has seen many decades in life shared this experience with me: she was in the checkout of her local grocery store, a common situation where someone can feel like a faceless number with flour, eggs, and broccoli on the endless conveyor belt. Among the items was a small bottle of chocolate milk for her grandson. The teenager bagging the groceries paused with the milk in hand, and looking directly at her said,

"Do you want to keep this out so you can drink it in the car?" That's likely what he would do. It just tickled her that the teen saw her as someone who might like some chocolate milk right away, as a teen would. She still smiles telling this story.

Even small gestures can help connect with each other's humanity. At a more invested level, helping others see the good means to stand up for your principles and stand up for others.

Have you ever been part of a group conversation at work that turns to gossip? Likely we all have. It's tempting to join in and be like the others. It's a little harder to remain silent, adhering to the adage that if you can't say anything good, don't say anything at all. The best approach is to defend the object of gossip. "It's possible they are taking a lot of sick days not to go skiing but because they're dealing with some difficult situation at home." Or stand up for others by shutting down the thread. "I'm not comfortable knocking someone who's not here to explain themself." In adhering to your principles, you'll also build respect. Who wouldn't want you on their side if the next time they are the ones being gossiped about?

Practice Compassion; Foster a Sense of Belonging

The feeling of belonging, to another or to a group, is one of the basic needs to be fulfilled for individuals to reach their potential. Psychologist Abraham Maslow described a hierarchy of needs in five levels in his motivational theory published in 1943.[8] There have been additions and criticisms through the years, but Maslow's hierarchy of needs remains a tool used in education, corporations, nonprofits, and many other areas.

The five levels of needs are depicted in colored layers of a pyramid, which makes the concept easy to visualize and understand. On the most basic level, physiological needs must be met. These are what is needed for physical survival, such as food, water, and shelter.

The next level to motivate human behavior is safety, which involves security and stability. The mid-level is love and belonging in relationships and feeling accepted.

Once that is achieved, individuals can fulfill the need for esteem, self-confidence, and respect, according to Maslow. Then finally the individual can reach the pinnacle of needs—self-actualization—which is reaching their potential.

Later psychologists postulated that the steps are fluid, not one necessary before the other. Expansions added cognitive, aesthetic, and transcendence needs.

For our purposes, I think it is helpful to consider the motivational needs in human behavior and recognize the importance of belonging. This powerful feeling can be satisfied within a family, school, club, religion, political party, or any of the many ways society brings people together.

While nurturing a feeling of belonging—which I think is particularly important for children—take care to not go so far as exclude anyone who doesn't "belong." Avoid feeding the mindset that everyone in group A is smart and good and those in group B are neither. This is where compassion comes in. And respect.

Being treated with respect helps people—adults, teens, and children—believe in themselves. They feel valued and loved.

A way to do this is with language. Researchers who have studied how respect gets translated through the words we use came up with 11 categories. Rephrasing words from a negative to a positive connotation helps develop a culture of respect. The categories are outlined in a *Psychology Today* article by Marilyn Price-Mitchell titled "The Language of Respect."[9] Her article is directed for "walking our talk with teenagers" but it is applicable to any age.

- **Encouragement.** Instead of complaining when someone feels discouraged, let them know you admire their ability to overcome tough challenges. Instead of dismissing painfully felt struggles with a bromide such as "Cheer up!" (that never works) or trying to make everything right, you are showing support and faith in the person.

The Top Five Qualities of Respectfulness

- **Grace.** Avoid blaming; separate the person from their behavior. Forgive them for any mistakes and give them the chance to get it right. For example, "I know you are not the same as your mistake."
- **Guidance.** Don't just hope a person will find their way through it all. Helpful words might be "There is no such thing as a dumb question."
- **Respect.** Rather than a singular focus of success, such as good grades, exceeding sales goals, or finishing a 10K, build an overall appreciation for setting goals and putting effort into achieving them. It's about the effort.
- **High expectations.** When someone falls short—and inevitably we all will at one time or another—try to encourage them to pursue and envision goals that are important to them. Not what others might want for them.
- **Hope.** Instead of putting your own imprint on trying to help someone get through a difficult day, help them picture a better tomorrow using their best qualities. Assure them that they have the wherewithal to cope.
- **Love.** This is a big one! Don't just speak to the minds; speak also to the hearts.
- **Relationship.** Use words that build connection through sharing. "I want to know how you felt when ... ."
- **Understanding.** Don't make assumptions. Tap into perspective through empathy. "I've never been through that—what was it like for you?"
- **Unity.** Foster an environment of cooperation and collaboration. It's not "my way or the highway" anymore.
- **Accountability.** Hold everyone accountable for creating and adhering to a culture of respect, no matter whether it's at work, home, or out in the world.

Words matter. They can pierce, they can soothe. The way they come together is entirely under your control. Choose and use the right words that bring people of different cultures and beliefs together in bonding for the common good. Only through accepting other views and beliefs, without having to mark them wrong or right and thus denigrate or defend, can we begin to appreciate our role in the human panoply of life.

Acknowledge the Dignity of Human Life, No Matter One's Station, Culture, or Preferences

Award-winning author Allia Zobel Nolan puts it this way: one doesn't have to be a king or queen or celebrity or million-dollar athlete to qualify for respect.

> *Allia Zobel Nolan is the author of over 150 traditionally published titles. Her books reflect her main passions: God and cats. Recent titles include* Heavenly Headbutts: Reflections of Hope about Cats and Eternity, The Worrywart's Prayer Book, Laugh Out Loud: 40 Women Humorists Celebrate Then and Now ... Before We Forget, *and most recently* Why Can't My Brother Be More Like My Cat? *with art by New York Times bestselling illustrator Lee Wildish.*
>
> *Her books have won numerous Indie Awards, the Catholic Media Award, and the Zibby Book Award.*
>
> *A former Reader's Digest Children's Publishing Senior Editor, Nolan also writes humor and general lifestyle pieces for various online newspapers and magazines. She lives and writes in New England with her husband, two cats, and a puppy mill rescue dog named Miss Kitty.*

"I respect people who have the courage of their convictions, who are not swayed by the baying of the crowd," she explained. "My mother loved the saying 'To thine own self be true.' It's difficult, especially in the world we live in, to be steadfast and not wishy-washy. But respect to me is when I look up to someone or aspire to be like them because they are living a simple life well."

This brings us back to the eighteenth-century philosopher Immanuel Kant with his radical, at the time, notion that every single person deserved respect by the very fact they are human beings. No one had to buy their way into respect, nor was it limited to the noble class or the educated.

Former US Education Secretary Miguel Cardona sees respect as bigger than any one person or title. "It's just humanity, right? I really go back to that. It's just treat people like we're all the same. It doesn't matter, titles or letters after your name. Oftentimes I'm reminded of that because I get treated differently sometimes when people find out who I am," he said.

"Or they'll walk by my wife and forget to say hi to her, but then come to me and I'm like, 'Ah, you know, you're going to get the treatment based on how you treated my wife, not me.'"

"The dignity of human life" is a lofty phrase. Our challenge is to translate that into concrete actions. What can you do to honor one's dignity?

A simple act, which costs not a penny, is to say their name. Greet them by name. It's an honored way of saying, "I see you." Our names are personal.

Along that line, spell someone's name correctly. A Smith could be a Smyth. When sending an email or text, quick ways of communicating, the impulse is to go for a common spelling or how you think a name is spelled. Take a moment, though, to look up the spelling by using the search function on earlier emails or go to a company or organization's website. Get it right. It is important to the person you're communicating with.

I keep going back to a passage in David Brooks's 2023 book *How to Know a Person: The Art of Seeing Others Deeply and Being Deeply Seen.*[10] It is a passage worth rereading: "If you consider that each person has a soul, you will be aware that at the deepest levels we are all equals. We're not equal in might, intelligence, or wealth, but we are all equal on the level of our souls," Brooks wrote. "If you see the people you meet as precious souls, you'll probably wind up treating them well."

■ ■ ■

As mentioned previously, the qualities of being a respectful person are not limited to the five I mentioned. Let people know you appreciate them and their efforts. At work, take a moment to say something detailed like "Great job getting that report done so well on deadline." Or send an email expressing appreciation.

Be cognizant of another person's time they are giving you. Do not waste it. Respond in a timely manner to their requests.

Emphasize someone's strengths, not their weaknesses. This is true for children, spouses, other family members, friends, and colleagues. Even casual acquaintances. You will be perceived as the better person for it.

Admit when you're wrong. Apologize. Resist blaming another for your mistakes. Speak directly with someone, never behind their back. Speak up if someone else is being disrespectful. Call them out in a firm, direct way but not harshly.

MaryLou Pagano, the executive director of The Sheen Center, was faced with this situation. A performer had publicly criticized a staff member for lower-than-expected attendance at her event. When Pagano heard about it, she knew she would have to speak to the performer, even though the event was over. She had an obligation to her staff.

"I have to deal with this today," she told me when we were chatting about this book. "It's part of the fiber of how we treat each other in the office." She couldn't ignore the disrespectful treatment to her staff, but she also did not want to disparage the performer.

"I will say to her, 'I'm sorry, but why were you upset when you got here? How can I offer to make your experience better next time?' It's worth it to me to not come at it with hand on hip and make the other person defensive.

"As a last resort, I'm willing to give it the old college try to be respectful."

> ### Think About It
>
> 1. What qualities do you consider important for respectfulness?
> 2. How do you handle situations when someone else has views opposite yours? Could you handle it better?
> 3. What small acts can you do at work or in everyday life to honor individual dignity?

CHAPTER 6

Respectfulness at Work

Respect is how to treat everyone, not just those you want to impress.
— Richard Branson

Indra K. Nooyi exudes respectfulness, in her no-nonsense way, and in turn is widely respected. Such respect did not come automatically to her, no matter how high her corporate positions. A native of India, she was the first immigrant and woman of color to run a Fortune 50 company, PepsiCo. She led the company to reinvent itself with healthier products and environmental sensibilities, all while motivating employees. She did this with purpose.

Healthier products for a company based on sugary soft drinks that also owned Lay's potato chips? Yes, she showed the way, for instance by hiring scientists to devise new formulas to meet the changing priorities of customers.

She created three imperatives for the PepsiCo organization under the umbrella of performance with purpose: "*Nourish* humanity and the communities in which we live, *replenish* our environment, and *cherish* the people in our company," she wrote in her fascinating autobiography, *My Life in Full*.[1]

> *Indra Nooyi consistently has ranked among the world's 100 most powerful women.* Fortune *magazine placed her second in its Most Powerful Women List of 2015.*[2] *Other lists include those by* Forbes, Time *magazine, and the* Wall Street Journal.
>
> *She joined PepsiCo in 1994 as its senior vice president for strategic planning and became the CEO in 2006, a position she held until 2019 along with the title of chairman.*
>
> *After leaving PepsiCo, Indra was appointed by Governor Ned Lamont to be the co-director of the newly created Connecticut Economic Resource Center, a public-private partnership with the Connecticut Department of Economic and Community Development.*
>
> *She has received 15 honorary degrees, including an honorary doctorate of humane letters from Yale University. The US State Department awarded her an Outstanding American by Choice and she was awarded the Padma Bhushan, India's third highest civilian honor.*

I've known Indra for many years. As a CEO she did a fantastic job. She knew where every nickel was buried and how it should be used. She moved PepsiCo into positive areas and she did that by the force of her personality. Since her time at PepsiCo, she has lent her business acumen to various corporate boards, such as Amazon and nonprofits.

Indra Nooyi never has anything bad to say about anybody or anything. That relates to her value of respectfulness. "In the workplace I had a perspective that universally everyone should be respected equally. Respectfulness should be a core tenet; it is not an option. It should be in the fabric of everything we do," she told me. "Treat everybody like you would like to be treated. Everybody wants to be treated with respect; it doesn't matter what their background is. You want everybody to be treated with respect."

To instill a culture of respect in the workplace, whether it's a multinational corporation like PepsiCo or a fledgling startup, the leaders have to model a respectful behavior. "There's no point telling people you've got to treat everybody with respect and then you end up treating people with disrespect. To me, that's the worst thing you can do. So you have to model the behavior, not once or twice—you've got to model it all the time. Consistently. It's very, very important.

"Now, if you start treating people with disrespect and then tell people you've got to treat people with respect, people are like 'give me a break! You should be the last person who should be giving us advice because you are so rude to people.'" Don't let that be you.

In this chapter you will hear from corporate leaders on how to nurture respectfulness, even within different cultures, experiences, and expectations. Conversely, they will tell you about the pitfalls to avoid.

■ ■ ■

Sol Trujillo is an executive on the international stage who embodies a balance of strength and sensitivity. In talking with Sol, if you don't know about his business successes, you will first notice his people-oriented perspective.

"People need to be respectful of the time and work that others do," he said when I asked him about cultivating respectfulness. "Be conscious of everyone's time and what their priorities are versus yours."

> *Solomon "Sol" Trujillo made his mark in the fields of global media communications and technology. He was the CEO of Telstra, US West, and Orange S.A., and was a trade policy advisor to both the Bill Clinton and George W. Bush administrations.*
>
> *(continued)*

> *At 32, Trujillo became the youngest executive in the history of AT&T. His "firsts" include being the first to lead three different $50 billion market cap companies in three continents. A native of Wyoming, he was the first US-born Latino to become the CEO of a Fortune 200 company (US West).*
>
> *President Clinton presented him the Ronald H. Brown Corporate Bridge Builder Award. Trujillo has served on a variety of boards, such as for PepsiCo, Target, Gannett, Bank of America, and many others.*

In business, you have to realize that everyone has their own priority in their lives. "Mine may not be yours," he said. Time is the variable, such as if raising children is one's priority. To be respectful, apologize if you have infringed on their time, for example, by being late to a meeting.

Trujillo is one of the most accomplished business executives I have ever met. I was advised, when we first met, that I should be very careful of Sol Trujillo because he was mindful of virtually everything and what everybody did. Well, I was pretty straight with him as I have been with all, and we have had a great working relationship over the years.

He is a very warm, engaging guy who has a point of view for the American consumer. He goes around the bend to solve problems for you and not offend anybody. Instead, he looks for ways to praise.

He likes to make lists. So when we were talking about respectfulness, he naturally responded with a list of three points. "Three things determine the notion of being respectful," he said.

1. "Time."
2. "Priority."
3. "Communicate with clarity the first two."

Be respectful of other people's time and know what their priorities are. "Be mindful, be attentive. Listen on a personal level," he said. "If you don't listen, the result is negative."

When you're young, you think you know everything, he said, recalling his own early career years. "As you get more experienced, you realize you don't know it all and you need to listen."

Along with listening, take care with your choice of words, how you articulate your thoughts. "It might seem good to be very direct, but that may come across as rude and not willing to listen."

Trujillo has run communications networks around the world in more than 30 countries. If someone needed advice on how to develop a network like that, Trujillo was the man to talk to.

He advises that in business you need to have a wider-angle lens than what you're born with. "If you're living a global business life, a big lesson is learning that not all live by the same standards and norms," he told me. "Doing business in Germany or France is different than the Far East and different than American or Western culture.

"It's always about understanding the environment, respecting how much time is required. Then, engage with both eyes," he said, mentioning an adage I will never forget. "You have two eyes, two ears, and one mouth. Use proportionally."

■ ■ ■

Frances Hesselbein had a saying: "Listen first, speak last." I bet she would have liked Sol Trujillo's adage. To lead with respectfulness, to be a great leader, you must listen to your employees. Ultimately, the tough decisions are yours, but people should first feel like they have been heard.

After Hesselbein met the management guru Peter Drucker in 1981 when she was CEO of the Girl Scouts, she learned that he had a similar saying: "Think first, speak last."

She liked this phrase so much that she made it an invisible tattoo, along with another of his sayings, "Ask, don't tell." She wrote about this in her essay "My Journey with Peter Drucker," included in the book *Work Is Love Made Visible*[3] (see Chapter 4).

"We need leaders who practice the art of listening," she wrote. "We need leaders who use listening to include, not exclude—to build consensus, appreciate differences, and find common concepts, common language, and common ground."

The art of listening implies discipline. You have to turn off the impulse to be forming a reply when someone else is talking. If you're talking—even if it's in your head—then you're not listening.

Listen to learn. No one has all the answers. This might sound convoluted, but you don't know what you don't know. Listen with an open mind to learn a different perspective or perhaps solution.

Peter Drucker famously advised that the most important thing in communication is hearing what isn't said.[4] To do that, you must listen intently. You must notice body language for clues that might not match the words spoken. You must listen with respect for what the other person is trying to communicate.

After getting to know Drucker and eventually carrying on his work through his nonprofit foundation, Hesselbein sometimes used his "Think first, speak last" advice interchangeably with her "Listen first, speak last." (See Chapter 5 for an exploration of active listening.)

Mark Twain had a memorable way of putting things, including the importance of listening. "If we were supposed to talk more than we listen," he said, "we would have two tongues and one ear."[5]

■ ■ ■

Respectfulness should be a goal unto itself, a virtue to cultivate, as we've been discussing. But in the business world you could also see a tangible benefit: retaining loyal employees.

Michael Dowling (whom you met in Chapter 4) said something surprising to me when we were talking about building a culture of respectfulness in the workplace. The CEO emeritus of Northwell Health, the largest private health network in New York with hospitals also in western Connecticut with 105,000 employees, said he pays no attention to educational degrees when hiring.

He said he couldn't care less "quite frankly where you got your degree. I couldn't care less what your grade point average is; I don't think it matters at all."

What does matter? One word: *attitude*.

"I like to hire for attitude, for positive attitude," he said. "I like to hire people who want to believe they can do something good and have a sense of positivity about the community. They want to make the place better. It's all about values and behaviors."

Dowling speaks of these corporate values when he meets with new employees. And he does this every Monday. Yes, *every Monday*. As you can imagine with an enterprise as extensive as Northwell Health, every week he sees hundreds of new employees.

"We hire about 300 people a week and I meet them all and spend quite a bit of time on the issues of decency and respect and honesty and how we deal with and relate to one another. How we communicate with one another, how we respect one another's opinions.

"How we can have respectable disagreement, and you know it's central to the culture we try to create inside of Northwell," he said. "But it is also central to the societal culture. What kind of community do you want to be in?"

Not surprisingly, at Northwell, Dowling says, turnover rates are low.

"People stay with us a long time and if you walk around any of our hundreds and thousands of facilities and ask people why they like working here, they will, I believe, overall tell you it's because they feel respected."

■ ■ ■

As leaders, you have an influence on many people and, of course, you have to know how to handle a variety of situations and personalities with equal aplomb. Cultivate respectfulness; be watchful for disrespect.

"There's an error of omission and an error of commission. You can be respectful to people, but if other people are disrespectful and you don't call them out on it, then you're committing an error of omission and you should watch out for that," Nooyi said.

Here's how she would handle it: if you see someone being disrespectful, stop them right there, pull them aside and say, "Hey, can I understand why there's so much disrespect going on here?"

Such behavior plays out, for example, in a meeting when someone is presenting and somebody cuts them off. "Right then you call them out and say, 'Could you let her finish?' or 'Could you let him finish?' Do it right there, but not in a way that hurts people. They'll clam up and won't see it as constructive. Do it in such a way that's constructive."

Standing up for the one disrespected has to be done as quickly as possible.

"Because if you forget to do it later, that's the worst kind because now you send a message to the whole company or to the entire work group that it's okay to be rude and disrespectful. It's tolerated. Or if you're the pet of the leader, it's tolerated," she said. "You don't want any of that."

■ ■ ■

Let's drill down to find what builds respectfulness in the workplace. As we've noted, respect is neither automatic nor evenly applied. A starting point—and this is essential—is trust.

Employees have to trust their leaders to make the right decisions and to treat everyone fairly. Leaders have to trust their employees to operate at their best. And everyone within the organization has to trust each other to be working toward company goals and to not undermine each other to get ahead.

There are steps to take to create this sort of environment, a place where people want to come to work and invest their careers. Those new to leadership—and undoubtedly even some who have been at it a number of years—might think the first step is to project strength. Not so.

In the *Harvard Business Review* article "Connect, Then Lead,"[6] the three authors explore behavioral science for qualities to establish true leadership.

Amy J. C. Cuddy, an assistant professor of business administration at Harvard Business School at the time of the 2013 article, with Matthew Kohut and John Neffinger, industry consultants and coauthors of the book *Compelling People: The Hidden Qualities That Make Us Influential*, said Niccolò Machiavelli had it only half right when he postulated that because it was difficult be both feared and loved as a leader, it was better to be feared.

Research now shows, they wrote, that "when we judge others—especially our leaders—we look first at two characteristics: how lovable they are (their warmth, communion, or trustworthiness) and how fearsome they are (their strength, agency or competence)."

People who are judged to be competent but lack warmth often draw envy of others, which may involve respect but lead to resentment. Conversely, people judged as warm but incompetent elicit pity, which can result in them becoming marginalized.

These reactions would seem to support Machiavelli's perspective. But—and this is important—it's *not* an either–or dichotomy. The key is to develop one characteristic first, then the other. First warmth, then strength. Does that surprise you? Are you thinking that warm-fuzzy leaders don't get the job done? Read on.

"Leaders who project strength before establishing trust run the risk of eliciting fear, and along with it a host of dysfunctional behaviors. Fear can undermine cognitive potential, creativity and problem solving and cause employees to get stuck and even disengage."

I have seen this happen. Maybe the CEO, or mid-level manager, who bellows across the room, "Why isn't that report done yet?" gets action. Maybe, for a while, production is up. But not for long.

The way to lead with lasting influence is to start with warmth. "Prioritizing warmth helps you connect immediately with those around you, demonstrating that you hear them, understand them and can be trusted by them," the coauthors write.

This doesn't mean you have to start baking cookies for the office or pick up doughnuts on the way to the headquarters. Warmth can be projected through nonverbal signals, such as a nod or a smile, to show that you are attentive to their concerns, you are pleased to be where you are and not distracted by the next thing you have to do or place to be.

A genuine smile can be contagious. We tend to mirror nonverbal expressions so when someone is emanating warmth or joy or amusement, we can't help but smile ourselves.

Notice this at the next cocktail party or office meeting: people unintentionally mimic others' gestures. If someone sweeps an arm in making a point, someone else will do the same in response. One person stands with hands in pockets, soon others do, too—if they have pockets! Such inadvertent mirroring indicates being in sync. It is reassuring.

The purest form I've seen is with babies. If you happen to smile at a baby, for example, one perched in a grocery store carriage, then that baby—with nothing to gain or lose or calculate—likely will spontaneously smile back. It's natural.

What if you consider yourself a grump, a curmudgeon, a serious person, more prone to scowling than smiling? You can't fake it.

An executive I once worked with had a bright, wide-open smile that made his eyes crinkle. He'd flash that smile when making a point. But then just as quickly, it was gone. It didn't fade, it was turned off. I couldn't help but think of a puppet. People in the room responded with unease.

If you are more grumpy than cheerful, you can train yourself to smile more. Think of a moment of joy or transcendent beauty. Or even of how good it will feel to take your shoes off when you get home. Let a small smile come from within.

As with so many gestures, authenticity matters. It is everything.

When trying to project warmth avoid going overboard. Too much enthusiasm by talking loudly or excitedly will fall flat, except perhaps when trying to motivate a sales force to reach goals. Otherwise, people will think you are indiscriminate in your attention. Or fake.

Try speaking with a lower pitch, lower volume, "that suggests that you're leveling with people—that you're sharing the straight scoop, with no pretense or emotional adornment. In doing so, you signal that you trust those you're talking with to handle things the right way."

You might share a personal story. Briefly. My advice is do this judiciously.

If any employee, or friend for that matter, comes to you with a problem, you might relate your own experience, which would indicate empathy and understanding. But don't take over the conversation and make it about you.

Brené Brown, a bestselling author, *Dare to Lead* podcaster, and research professor at the University of Houston, calls this *narrative takeover*. "Rather than being good stewards of a story, we hijack the story and center ourselves," she wrote in her 2021 book *Atlas of the Heart: Mapping Meaningful Connection and the Language of Human Experience*.[7] "That centering takes many different shapes, including shifting the focus to us, questioning or not believing what someone is sharing because it's different than our lived experience, or diminishing the importance of an experience because it makes us feel uncomfortable, or worse, complicit."

I am quite sure that you can summon examples of "narrative takeover" in conversations with family members, friends, or acquaintances. You're left feeling deflated, unheard. In the workplace, it can feed an unhealthy environment.

We readily recognize when someone else is taking over the conversation or story. But do you realize when you might be doing it? And why? The narrative takeover can be about "protecting our ego, behavior, or privilege. The less diverse our lived experiences, the more likely we are to find ourselves struggling with narrative takeover or narrative tap-out," Brown wrote. "Tap-out" implies subtle disinterest or flagrant tuning out. You're not truly listening, maybe mind wandering, eyes glazing over.

"If we had thought bubbles, they'd say 'This is too uncomfortable' or 'I don't care enough about you to care about this,' or 'I can't take this on right now.'"

I doubt that you would want to send the message that you don't care enough—no matter who is talking or what the issue might be. That's rude, disrespectful.

But if the tap-out is because you don't have time right then to jump in, then say so. It is better to be honest than to have your signals misinterpreted.

How to listen to build trust? "Like empathy, story stewardship is not walking in someone else's shoes; it's being curious and building narrative trust as they tell you about the experience of being in their own shoes," Brown wrote. "It's about believing people when they tell you what an experience meant to them. The far enemy of narrative trust is fueling narrative distrust and diminishing the humanity of others and ourselves."

To motivate employees to listen to your message and agree or buy into it, you must validate their feelings and concerns.

I recall a high-level executive who earned respect when she acknowledged the extreme anxiety of employees after a corporate takeover. She couldn't promise that no one's position would be affected, but she did promise to share information as soon as she received it about the future direction. In these times of frequent corporate mergers that change circumstances and culture—even in the corporation that is on the acquisition end—openness is critical.

Once you have established trust with warmth, you can build to lead with strength based on competence.

"Feeling in command and confident is about connecting with yourself," the coauthors of the article "Connect, Then Lead" write. "And when we are connected with ourselves, it is much easier to connect with others."[8]

Certain physical stances can bolster your self-confidence, and when practiced can become natural. For example, try power poses that are open (arms loose at your side, not crossed against your middle) and expansive (engage your core to reach your full height with shoulders back, don't slouch). Think of it as occupying your space with energy, not merely just being there.

Many of us have been brought up to demonstrate our competence through hard work. Even in elementary school, we learn that studying leads to good grades, which indicates competence. Those As add up! Or do they?

We want to see ourselves as skilled, as strong, and want others to perceive us that way, too. And so to respect us. Counterintuitively, putting competence first, without establishing trust, undermines leadership.

"Without a foundation of trust, people in the organization may comply outwardly with a leader's wishes, but they're much less likely to conform privately—to adopt the values, culture, and mission of the organization in a sincere, lasting way," the coauthors write.

Trust in the leaders and each other leads to openness, the exchange of ideas, and the opportunity to change attitudes for the better.

Part of building trust is to project warmth coupled with strength. It is natural that others will form a judgment of you, even subconsciously, before they judge what you're saying. You want to be heard. You want to cultivate a culture of respectfulness and to do so requires your actions to match your words. It is possible.

■ ■ ■

You might think that someone such as Indra Nooyi with her high leadership positions and pedigree of a master's from the Yale School of Management would automatically command respect. Not always so. In the workplace subtle forces might be fostering disrespect. This can happen with gender, age, physical disabilities, background, or other differences within the group.

"When you're the only woman in the boardroom or seats of power, you notice that when they talked to men in positions of power there's a heightened level of deference than when they were talking to me," Nooyi said. "So I had to outperform the men to earn their respect."

A lack of respect could be shown in ways obvious or subtle. Interrupting women when they're the ones talking. Rolling their eyes or smiling at each other knowingly. "This is the past. Nowadays, it's considered bad behavior and bad form to do that. But in those days when I came into the workplace women's opinions were pooh-pooed. It's happened to me too many times. But, you know, I want to focus on the 80% where everything went well, not the 20% where things were wrong.

"I worked hard to show them I was competent and they in turn gave me their respect and treated me in a respectful way."

Take a moment here for introspection. Have you, even inadvertently, been part of that 20%? Not just a man exchanging knowing looks with another when a woman spoke up at the conference room table, but also a woman sharing a dismissive glance to another. Or were those subtle signals coming when someone from a younger generation was speaking or someone from an ethnic background different than yours? Be aware. Don't let it happen. Don't participate.

"Unfortunately, it's not yet a level playing field, at least I haven't seen it as a level playing field, because we're always wondering, always looking to see if the woman is not up to snuff. But for the men we say, 'Oh, this person is totally up to it. We just assume that the women have to earn their place or earn their respect while men have the respect when they come in because of their gender.

"It's way better than it used to be, but trust me, it does rear its ugly head now and then."

What Nooyi was describing won't surprise many other women leaders, and maybe some men who have sensed it against themselves. Gender "lurked below the surface," though not openly acknowledged, former Meta executive Sheryl Sandberg wrote about the early years of her career in her bestseller *Lean In*.[9]

"I started to see differences in attitudes toward women," she wrote. "I started noticing how often employees were judged not by their objective performance, but by the subjective standard of how well they fit in."

Her TEDWomen Talk on how women can succeed in the workforce, titled "Why We Have Too Few Women Leaders," touched a nerve.[10] Though her talk was in 2010, it remains a topic of discussion and debate.

"We need to speak out, identify the barriers that are holding women back, and find solutions," she wrote. The situation isn't only male versus female; oftentimes women hold themselves back instead of actively participating in discussions and decisions, she said.

It isn't easy to speak out. "Anyone who brings up gender in the workplace is wading into deep and muddy waters. The subject itself is a paradox, forcing us to acknowledge differences while trying to achieve the goal of being treated the same," she wrote.[11]

But the feedback from her 14-minute TED presentation convinced her that "talking can transform minds, which can transform behaviors, which can transform institutions."

Sheryl points to Ken Chenault, who was CEO of American Express from 2001 to 2018, as a leader in trying to make things right, to model respectfulness to all. "Ken openly acknowledges that in meetings, both men and women are more likely to interrupt a woman and give credit to a man for an idea first proposed by a woman. When he witnesses either of these behaviors, he stops the meeting to point it out."

This is exactly what Nooyi was referring to.

Kelly McKenzie, the author you met in Chapter 3, understands what it feels like to be treated differently, to be underestimated professionally. "When someone talks over me, I immediately get my guard up," she said. "I see it as disrespectful."

She cites a time when she was the sole employee in the antique shop FROG, started by her mother, Frankie Robinson, in downtown Vancouver.

"A fellow asked us to sell his late mother's huge Asian collection. We were shocked when he showed no respect for any of the pieces she'd carefully gathered over a lifetime," McKenzie said. "He didn't help his cause when he dismissed our appreciation for her acumen by demanding we give him a quote on the spot. This lack of respect for not only his late mother but also our knowledge continued throughout our relationship. He cut us off by talking only about himself. It was appalling."

■ ■ ■

When you encourage shared values in the workplace and communicate them to your staff, your people, you have to follow through and demonstrate that not only do you believe what you are saying but also that will you act.

The day before Michael Dowling and I spoke about respectfulness, he had terminated one of his senior leaders. It was tough. This high-level executive was "very, very bright." But after about three months, he was let go. Why?

"Not because he wasn't good at his job," Dowling said. "He was terrible in interpersonal relationship skills. He made everybody around him feel bad. Therefore, he cannot be in the organization even though his business skill is excellent. His analytic skill is excellent—but he's an asshole to be around."

Dowling doesn't use that term lightly. He said he does have a "no-assholes rule" when it comes to creating a poisonous atmosphere at work. When a book by Robert I. Sutton, a Stanford University professor of management science, called *The No Asshole Rule: Building a Civilized Workplace and Surviving One That Isn't*,[12] based on his essay in the *Harvard Business Review*, came out in 2010 Dowling bought 350 copies and handed them out to all of his leadership team.

Incidentally, if you are first taken aback by the word *asshole* and consider it vulgar, read Sutton's explanation in the *Harvard Business Review*[13] of why he used it. "I was determined to use the word 'asshole' in the title because, to me, other words like 'jerk,' 'bully,' 'tyrant,' 'despot,' and so on are just euphemisms for what people really call those creeps. And when I have done such damage to people (indeed, all of us are capable of being assholes some of the time), that is what I call myself. I know the term offends some people, but nothing else captures the emotional wallop."

When Dowling distributed the book, he told his management team, "If you know somebody that works for you who fits those descriptions, get rid of them!"

Employees still refer to that book he gave them, along with his permission to act. "Because," Dowling explained, "when people like you and you respect people around you, people are more productive when they don't have to worry about other people undermining you."

Realistically, at the topmost level you might not get rid of bad attitudes 100%. But even 90% helps and sets a tone for the culture of respectfulness.

■ ■ ■

Ways to show respectfulness include letting people know you appreciate them. It can be as simple as saying something like, "Your comments at the meeting sparked a great discussion." Be specific, be genuine.

Emphasize someone's strengths, not their weaknesses, at least not publicly. Never talk behind their backs or engage in gossip. This pertains to not only leaders but also everyone in the organization.

Apologize when wrong. It can happen, no one is infallible. Respond in a timely manner if someone makes a request. In these days of instant communication, that can be difficult. Emails pile up and answering all could take a big chunk of the workday.

Sol Trujillo manages his inbox by having a separate email address for family members and business associates.

Others flag emails for a later response or move them to a get-back-to-today folder. Sometimes you will want to zip off a quick reply that you will respond in detail later that day, or week. People understand busy schedules. And they appreciate the respectfulness shown in the acknowledging of their email, text, or phone call.

Practice drawing out ideas, and not just from your management team. Talk with your customers, your vendors, your nonmanagement employees. Respect their views. In a meeting, if someone makes a suggestion and someone else dumps on it, you could say, "Wait a minute. Let's build on it."

You ultimately might not act on a given idea. But if people know that they can openly share ideas, you'll all be the better for it. With brainstorming, one mediocre idea can be the springboard to something great.

Indra Nooyi emphasizes the importance of making people feel their opinion is valuable.

"Don't make them feel like they're giving opinions and you don't really care and somebody is just asking for their opinion because they've been told 'You should get so-and-so's opinion.'

"I think there's a whole training that could be done on how to listen and how to deal with people with respect."

Building a culture of respectfulness is not easy or necessarily quick. There's a lot of moving parts—from projecting warmth, then strength, to listening deeply to not tolerating jerks in leadership. But a culture of respectfulness is vital to a successful business. Everyone has a role in it.

Think About It

1. What do you project first: strength or warmth?
2. Have you ever tried to take over a conversation at work, even inadvertently? How did that go?
3. How can you build trust in your workplace? Be specific.

CHAPTER 7

Respectfulness in Family and Personal Relationships

I'm not concerned with your liking or disliking me ... .
All I ask is that you respect me as a human being.
— Jackie Robinson

Sarah McArthur keeps visual reminders on her desk, below her computer screen, of what is important. The reminders are four "pretty old" gold-toned round coasters with felt on the back. Each carries a message: Integrity. Loyalty. Citizenship. Respect for others.

She held up the one about respect to show me. It reads: "Ethical persons respect human dignity, privacy and the right to self-determination of all people. They are courteous, prompt and decent. They provide others with information they need to make informed decisions about their own lives. They do not patronize, embarrass or demean."

Each category has to do with ethics. The coasters, at least that's what she thinks they are, were given to her many years ago by her mentor and dear friend, Frances Hesselbein.

"People change over time," McArthur said, "but these definitions remain."

Yes, they do, and I think they are completely relevant today. Respect for others strikes me as particularly apt for personal relationships. Be decent, respect human dignity and privacy, never demean another person. These can be touchstones on the path to respectfulness within our families, to our closest friends, and to acquaintances.

In this chapter you will learn how to put respectfulness into actions, including how to argue, and to inculcate the value of being respectful into your children. And much more.

McArthur is the dynamic editor in chief of *Leader to Leader*,[1] an online and print journal founded in 1996 by Frances Hesselbein, who was leading The Peter F. Drucker Foundation for Nonprofit Management. Peter Drucker had convinced Hesselbein to guide the foundation and subsequently to start the journal, and she cultivated McArthur to follow in the position. The quarterly magazine features articles from various leaders on a range of topics related to management and, you guessed it, leadership. McArthur was a co-editor on the book *Work Is Love Made Visible*[2] with Hesselbein and Marshall Goldsmith, an executive coach and author whose publications include three *New York Times* bestsellers. The book is a compilation of essays about the "power of finding your purpose from the world's greatest thought leaders."

Sarah McArthur has more than two decades in publishing as a writer, editor, and writing coach. Her fields of expertise are management, leadership, and executive and business coaching.

She is editor in chief of Leader to Leader *journal and advisory board member of the Frances Hesselbein Leadership Forum in the Johnson Institute for Responsible Leadership at the University of Pittsburgh's Graduate School of Public and International Affairs (GSPIA).*

Author and editor of numerous books and articles including Work Is Love Made Visible *and* Coaching for Leadership,

> McArthur is a founding member of Marshall Goldsmith's 100 Coaches and former chief operating officer of Marshall Goldsmith, Inc.
>
> She holds a masters in publishing from George Washington University and a BA in English and Environmental Studies from the University of Oregon.

The essays are organized under headings such as "Leadership Is a Matter of How to Be, Not How to Do," "Defining Moments," and "Bright Future!" I particularly appreciate the Foreword by Alan Mulally, the former CEO of Boeing and Ford, whom I have known for many years. When he became head of the Ford Motor Company in 2006 he stepped into an enormous challenge: turn around the storied car manufacturer that was on the verge of bankruptcy with multibillion-dollar losses. That's *billion*. What kind of leadership skills would it take?

Mulally could inspire others. He didn't issue edicts, though he certainly could have. He could have been a task-oriented leader and gotten the job done. Instead, he was people-oriented and involved others at every level and every function in decisions—including customers. They had to understand the vision and feel optimistic about the company.

"Everyone is part of the team and everyone's contribution is respected, so everyone should participate," he said.[3] Within three years Ford was posting profits.

In the Foreword Mulally mentions lessons taught by his parents, which we would do well to extrapolate for guides toward acting with respectfulness in relationships. "The purpose of life is to love and be loved, in that order. ... Seek to understand before seeking to be understood. ... Respect everyone, we are all creatures of God, and worthy to be loved." He developed principles and practices through work. Apt for our purpose are: "Respect, Listen, Help, and Appreciate

Each Other. Have Fun ... Enjoy the Journey and Each Other ... and No Humor at Another's Expense."[4]

■ ■ ■

McArthur recalled the first time she and Hesselbein had lunch together. It was in 2011 at the Four Seasons Restaurant in New York City. (In Chapter 3, you met Alex von Bidder, a partner and manager of the famed restaurant.) As they talked about life, work, and purpose, Hesselbein asked McArthur this question: "What is it you see when you look out the window that is visible but not yet seen by others?" This became Hesselbein's signature question, which she posed to many.

"This question, so profound and provocative, requires us to explore our deepest thoughts, concerns, fears, and hopes for our society," McArthur wrote in her Preface to the book.

Your answer, unique to you, brings you to identifying your purpose. This knowledge when you act on it feeds self-respect, which as we have noted before is necessary for truly treating others respectfully.

McArthur and I chatted recently and in that hour she frequently referred to lessons learned from her mentor, Hesselbein, whom I had known for many years, until her death in 2022 at the astonishing age of 107.

Frances Richards Hesselbein began her work as a reluctant volunteer Girl Scout troop leader in her native Pennsylvania—she was the mother of a young son—and rose to become the CEO of Girl Scouts of the USA for 13 years, taking it from the Betty Crocker era to a diverse organization with a membership of 3 million girls.

She then headed the Leader to Leader Institute, which had been called the Peter F. Drucker Foundation for Nonprofit Management Foundation. It became known as the Frances

Hesselbein Leadership Institute and later was renamed the Frances Hesselbein Leadership Forum; it is now part of the University of Pittsburgh Graduate School for Public and International Affairs.

Hesselbein was a co-editor of 30 books in 30 languages, received 21 honorary doctoral degrees, and traveled to 68 countries representing the United States. President Bill Clinton awarded her the Presidential Medal of Freedom; in 2015 Fortune *magazine named her one of the World's 50 Greatest Leaders.*

Hesselbein was extremely active on boards. Everybody sought her opinion; she had connections it seemed to everybody in the United States. I was told when I came on a nonprofit board with her to "listen to Frances—she knows what she's talking about." This is the kind of reputation you would do well to emulate.

We used to meet for lunch, maybe once every other month when she was living in Manhattan, and we always had a great time together, talking about what was happening in the country and how everything could be affected. Even at her late age, she would walk, not taxi, from her place on 56th Street and on to First Avenue, Park Avenue, and 52nd—to the Four Seasons—and you could see the steam coming off her as she walked through the door. She was energetic.

I remember when Hesselbein crossed the 100-year mark. I said to her, "Frances, most people don't make it to 100." She replied, "Well, I'm going to make it a lot further than that." And she did. To 107! And, amazingly, she literally worked up until the final minutes of her life. She really was exceptional.

McArthur recalled a 2012 TED Talk that Hesselbein had given in which she described an early lesson in respect for all people. Her defining moment at eight years old came from her grandmother, whom she called Mama Wicks.

"Mama Wicks had this beautiful living room with a full-size pipe organ, high ceilings, stained glass windows. In the room were two Chinese vases. Frances wanted to touch them; Mama Wicks said 'no, Frances, no one can touch them,'" McArthur recounted. "Mama Wicks took her by the hand and said, 'Let me tell you a story about the vases.'"

A Chinese man who did the laundry one day told Mama Wicks he was leaving the country. He missed his family, whom he was unable to bring over. He gave Mama Wicks the two beautiful vases. She asked why.

"'In my entire 10 years here, the little boys would chase me, call me names, and pull my queue. You are the only person who has ever called me Mr. Yee,' he replied. And Frances cried and cried and cried for Mr. Yee," McArthur said. "For the rest of her life she taught us respect for all people, across the sectors, across ages, across genders, across the parties, across the world she taught us about respect for all people. That is her legacy."

In an essay Hesselbein wrote for *Work Is Love Made Visible* titled "Be Positive!,"[5] she quoted an anonymous author:

> Be careful of your thoughts, for your thoughts become your words. Be careful of your words, for your words become your deeds. Be careful of your deeds, for your deeds become your habits. Be careful of your habits, for your habits become your character. Be careful of your character, for your character becomes your destiny.

■ ■ ■

Phil Gramm, the former senator from Texas, emphasized to his children and grandchildren that what they say is important. The words they choose can carry lasting meaning. "You need to think before you say things because once it comes out of your mouth, it's hard to put it back," he told them.

Respectfulness in Family and Personal Relationships

"How many people start arguing with their spouse over something. And they say something, and their spouse says something. They say something, she says something and pretty soon they don't even remember what the argument was about," Gramm noted in our conversation on respectfulness. "But they remember what the other one said and how they said it."

Feelings are hurt. No one wins.

Gramm has a good rule of thumb. "I don't say things to people that I wouldn't want them to say to me. I may think it, but I try not to say it." Self-discipline. "It just doesn't help to say it, especially when you're dealing with people you love and live with."

There is a way to argue respectfully, to stand up for yourself and articulate your points. Don't raise your voice; yelling only escalates the conflict. Step away, if you must, to diffuse the situation. A quick walk can do wonders.

But avoid resorting to the silent treatment. We all know what that means because I wager at some point we have been either at the giving or the receiving end of it. Neither feels good.

The silent treatment descends like a heavy dark curtain when one person gets so upset they can't process their emotions or express them in a respectful way. So they turn off and ignore the other. Maybe they pretend nothing is wrong or more likely they want you to figure out what it is and apologize.

The situation gets passive-aggressive and over time can give resentment space to grow. This can become a pattern among family members or between spouses. It's hard to break a pattern once it becomes a familiar way of dealing with differences or anger. We tend to take on expected roles, without much—if any—thought. Consider family dynamics and how in response to the slightest friction an otherwise competent corporate manager regresses into the "baby" as siblings assume their parts.

But patterns can be broken. It takes awareness and resolve. Recognize what buttons are being pushed and hold back from reacting emotionally, fueled by long-ago slights.

There's a better way to handle arguments. Once you've regained self-control, say that you want to discuss the differences and understand where the other person is coming from. Stay in the present, don't dredge up past grievances. It's hard to tap into respectfulness but try, and the outcome will be better.

"Disagreeing is not a reason to be disrespectful," Gramm said.

■ ■ ■

If you're in the office when a disagreement happens, then take some deep breaths to regain control of your emotions and refocus. Criticize the behavior, not the person.

Jefferson Fisher, a trial lawyer in Texas, has cultivated a sizable social media audience by teaching people how to have tough conversations, whether it's in personal relationships or in business. With nearly six million followers on Instagram, it appears people are hungry for this information. He has a podcast and his first book, *The Next Conversation: Argue Less, Talk More*, was published in 2025. Oprah Winfrey featured an article by Jefferson in her *Oprah Daily* electronic newsletter, "The 3 Golden Rules for Starting a Tough Conversation," an endorsement that guarantees attention.[6]

Fisher's advice is succinct and clear, as noted in a *New York Times* business section profile.[7] Before you begin your tough or sensitive conversation, think about how you will frame it, he said. "No. 1, you tell the person the issue you want to talk about. Two, you say how you want to feel after the conversation. That's very important because you're inserting the goal. Now I know what you want to talk about. I know the conversation is going to be done when this goal has been achieved. And three, you get their buy-in into the frame."

I can see the value in his approach. Think how often we (or the other person) start a tough talk brimming with emotion, ramble around and maybe cast accusations, and the point gets lost. We create a confrontation, not a conversation.

Respectfulness in Family and Personal Relationships

Fisher said a mistake couples make is thinking the first conversation about an issue is the last. "The bigger the issue, the more conversations that are needed," he said.

I think it helps to know a decision doesn't have to be immediate. You allow time for reflecting, evaluating, and for forming a response. You are showing respectfulness for the other's views, even though you disagree.

That sounds quite civil, doesn't it? But arguments rarely are felt like civil discussions. And it can seem counter to say this, but sometimes an out-and-out argument actually feels good. Fisher calls this the "feel-good hormone"—dopamine—which motivates and rewards.

When someone is rude or insulting, they are seeking something from you. A reaction. "Their search for dopamine has little to do with you personally," Fisher said in his book.[8] Instead, it's generally a reflection of their own insecurities.

"Belittling others can make the powerless feel powerful, the ignored feel seen, and the jealous feel like they've gained something," he said. They get a dose of dopamine from their sense of control over your negative reaction. Their temporary "high" comes at your expense. Don't trigger it!

See the insults or belittling for what they are—attempts to elicit a response. "Remember, it's not about you. It's about their need for your response," Fisher said.

That sounds logical, but in the heat of the moment when someone is calling you a jerk or worse, it's hard to think rationally and stay calm.

Try these strategies to deflect:

♦ Give a long pause. Let their words echo back to them. The silence might seem awkward, but that's okay. It shows that you are the one with control.

- Slowly repeat what they said. The key is to say the words s-l-o-w-l-y so they hear each one as they fall flat. Or, matter-of-factly, not heatedly, ask them to repeat what they said.
- Keep breathing fully. Shallow breathing makes you tense; breathing deep is calming. You might need it.

Whatever approach you take, avoid escalating the situation. It's not worth it.

■ ■ ■

It's impossible for everyone to agree on everything. You foster respectfulness in your relationships when you disagree by enunciating your points, not by putting the other person down for spouting an opposing view.

"Respect is listening, thinking, managing my emotions when I'm conversing with someone or relating with someone I don't agree with," McArthur told me. "Sometimes I have to slow it way down so I don't get heated in conversation."

She taught herself to be careful with adjectives when speaking. Adjectives? Sure, they can be overused and may be unnecessary; for example, you don't need to say "giant mountain"—but why would she avoid them?

"As soon as I slap an adjective before that noun, I'm setting my communication up for conflict, for disagreement," she said. "If I say 'blue tree,' I'm relating to some and not others. A lot of times to maintain communications, I'll just say 'tree' and let people think of their own kind of tree. That's one of my ways of having respect for people, by letting them figure it out for themselves."

There is a way, she told me, to use words to express thoughts, ideas, opinions without demeaning those who disagree. It takes a lot of strength and courage.

"I call it *deliberance*. Which isn't exactly a word, but when I say it, what I mean is that I am being deliberate *on purpose*. It's thinking about what I'm saying, what others are saying, carefully before responding," McArthur said.

Respectfulness in Family and Personal Relationships

Deliberance also translates to evaluating your actions. "Respect for others really has a lot to do with managing myself. If I look at the timeline of my own life, the external circumstances that have occurred during my lifetime, how have I acted and reacted? How have I handled myself to be respectful and stand up for what I believe in, which is respect for all people?"

Such self-reflection can be beneficial to your growth and knowledge. Former Education Secretary Miguel Cardona has seen his share of people disagreeing—it would be unusual to be in a White House Cabinet-level position and *not* see it.

"There are times when it's been difficult to maintain a posture of respect when being disrespected," he said. "That's a personal decision I have to make. That goes back to my basic upbringing: treat others the way you want to be treated. If someone treats you badly, that doesn't mean *you* treat *them* badly.

"Obviously, you don't want to be in a situation where people are treating you badly, but you always have the option to treat people respectfully, despite not being respected."

Betsy McCaughey said when she's feeling disrespected, she doesn't show that she's upset. Or at least tries not to. "I kind of rise above it," she said. "I say that for two reasons. One is that I generally expect to see the other person again. And secondly, I often assume that the other person doesn't really know how offensive he or she is being."

As a cable news talk show host, she likely faces situations like that more than most of us. I asked whether she points out to the other person that their remarks are offensive. "Not usually," she said, with a laugh. "But maybe that's my shortcoming in life. I just move on."

She's got a point. You need balance: sometimes the disrespect calls for standing up for yourself and sometimes it's more productive to shrug it off and carry on with life.

■ ■ ■

Standing up for *others* is another matter. You've heard the expression in business that leaders need to "walk the talk." Hesselbein did that. She didn't just talk about respect; she showed and defended it.

At a luncheon in New York City around 2008, she had just given a speech and was sitting at a table with young gentlemen, executive-level leaders. "They were talking about the current president [of the United States] in the most derogatory terms," McArthur told me. "She listened for about five minutes then said, 'You can disagree, but not disrespect. You do not disrespect the highest leader in the highest office in the land; this is absolutely not what we do, this is not respect for all people.' She stood up, walked away, and didn't go back."

Her principled action affected them. One of the men chased after her, apologized for offending Hesselbein, and said she was right.

"It takes a lot of courage, a lot of love, to stand up, to say something," McArthur said. "To communicate in such a way that the words you're using are not demeaning, degrading, or name-calling."

The words you choose reflect your values and your integrity.

■ ■ ■

Relationships, whether within a family; with a spouse, friends, colleagues; or even casual acquaintances, such as neighbors, are vital to health and might even affect longevity. We would do well then to nurture them with respectfulness and not take people for granted.

"Love and belonging are irreducible needs for all people," research Professor Brené Brown said in her book, *Atlas of the Heart: Mapping Meaningful Connection and the Language of Human Experience*,[9] which was developed into a five-part series for HBO Max in 2022. As you saw in Chapter 5, belonging is so powerful that it is one of the steps on Maslow's hierarchy of needs, meaning that one must feel the security of belonging—to a person, family, group; there are many ways—in order to reach the pinnacle of self-actualization.

But succumbing to the pressure to fit in for the sake of belonging will not work in the long run. You will lack the deeper connection of shared humanity, which ought to arise with belonging. "True belonging doesn't require us to change who we are; it requires us to be who we are," Brown said. "We can never truly belong if we are betraying ourselves, our ideals, or our values in the process."

It's interesting, isn't it, how so much of our conduct and relationships circles back to that foundation of self-respect. Showing respectfulness in personal relationships means giving those relationships priority in your day-to-day busy life. How many times have you thought of a friend, but chores, schedules, obligations, the details of life occupy hour after hour and before you know it a week has gone by. Then a month. Then several months. As a result, you feel out of touch and it's harder to call or break the ice with an email or text.

Make a commitment to your friendship. Communicate, in some way, even if it's to say your schedule is packed, but you want them to know that you're thinking of them. Share what's going on in your life. Focus on the quality, not necessarily the quantity, of communication.

I had a friend who made a practice of checking in with friends, people he didn't want to lose touch with, every few months. One time it might be a former colleague, the next a long-ago school mate. If you were on the receiving end of this out-of-the-blue call from a busy person, you felt special.

Be there when they need support, even if "there" isn't in person. Call, send an e-card, or better yet, a handwritten note. Be empathetic; convey your concern. Resist the urge to tell them how they ought to fix the problem or situation. Be respectful of their abilities.

And let your friends know when you're the one who could use support; people like to be needed. (Barbra Streisand sang a popular song in the mid-1960s from the Broadway play "Funny Girl" with the lyrics "People who need people are the luckiest people in the world.") It doesn't have to be over a crisis; it could be a simple request for advice on how to limit your child's electronic screen time. Let yourself be vulnerable—no one is perfect—and above all, be real.

Nurture your friendships. Schedule time for a lunch, a walk, or even a 15-minute conversation. It's good for you!

Dr. Robert Waldinger, a psychiatry professor at Harvard Medical School, oversees the longest-running study on human wellness; it began with previous researchers in 1938. What has the ongoing study found to be one of the biggest factors in well-being as people age? Strong relationships.[10]

"The clearest message that we get from this 75-year study is this: good relationships keep us happier and healthier. Period," he said in a TED Talk in 2015, one of the most watched with 40 million views as of 10 years later.

"Strong, long-term relationships with spouses, family and friends built on deep trust—not achievement, not fortune or fame—were what predicted well-being," Susan Dominus wrote of the study in a 2025 article for *New York Times magazine* titled "How Nearly a Century of Happiness Research Led to One Big Finding."[11]

"We have this innate reluctance to socially connect, particularly with strangers—and then we're happier when we make ourselves," Waldinger said. "I find it a really useful thing to know."

■ ■ ■

One of the most important things we can do within personal relationships is to model respectfulness to children. They learn much more by watching what we do, rather than by what we say. As we've noted previously in this book, the paradigm has shifted, and ordering children to respect their elders doesn't hold meaning for them anymore. Age doesn't automatically confer respect.

Indra Nooyi, the former CEO of PepsiCo, also notes cultural differences. "I believe this whole notion of respect is cultural," she told me. "Respect coming from the culture I did in India is very different than the culture of respect when people come to the US.

"For example, we have incredible respect, and therefore respectfulness, for parents and our teachers and for elders because we believe they have the wisdom of age. You do your best not to hurt their feelings, you listen to them carefully. You give them enough leeway for their opinion, you don't mentally dismiss it immediately. You provide some allowance to know that they have been through a lot and they know a lot. You don't interrupt the parents and teachers and elders. You are grateful to them for the time they give imparting knowledge to you, nurturing you, developing you. That is the cultural environment I was brought up in."

Fast-forward to Nooyi coming to the United States. "The definition of respectfulness is different here," she said. "Respectfulness is respecting somebody's opinion. Having to listen to it is good, but pushing back, sometimes quite aggressively, interrupting somebody and saying 'Hey, excuse me, I don't buy into this.'

"And it was liberating in many ways. Now, I'm not passing an opinion about one culture or the other. I'm just observing. However, these are healthy conflicts to have in your mind," she said.

Her observations get to the heart of the philosophical debate on whether respect is innate with being a human, or is earned by virtue of age, accomplishments, or conduct. Either way, we have a responsibility to teach children how to lead respectful lives whether it's in the family or on the playground.

Alex von Bidder, the partner and manager of the Four Seasons restaurant whom you met in Chapter 3, was the gatekeeper to the best tables for celebrity, political, and business movers and shakers, but he made it his mission to teach children. Once a year, beginning in 2006, the restaurant held Children's Day in which kids aged five to 14 dined for free—from the regular menu. No food fights, no jumps into the water in the Pool Room, as more than 400 children were served some of New York's finest cuisine.

"We're honoring them with respect, and treating them as if they're grown-ups," von Bidder told the *New York Times* during a lunch in 2010.[12] "The young have been influenced by a noticeable decline in adults' manners since the Four Seasons opened," he noted.

He decided to help further with manners by writing a delightful book called *Wiggins Learns His Manners at the Four Seasons Restaurant*.[13] The story follows a chocolate Labrador puppy named Wiggins through a manners class at the restaurant. Of course, he's a rambunctious puppy, which gets him into a bit of trouble. Among the 10 lessons are "When you meet someone, shake his or her paw and look him or her in the eye when you introduce yourself," and "It is polite to listen patiently when someone is talking, but it's even better to show interest by paying attention and asking questions," and "Always ask before you take something that doesn't belong to you. Before you do something you shouldn't, slow down and think before you act."

The charming drawings by Leslie McGuirk are punctuated with humorous asides. (For example, the oldest and wisest dog in Manhattan is named Chi-waa-waa and sits on a red and gold throne of sorts above a sign "Spiritual Advice Given; Wait Your Turn" while other dogs are quietly chanting ommm nearby.) I love it when a book you're reading to a child is also entertaining for an adult.

■ ■ ■

Developing the capacity for respect is a lifelong challenge, wrote Dr. Bruce Duncan Perry in an article on respect for Scholastic's *Early Childhood Today*.[14]

"As with adults, young children build their sense of self-respect from their interactions with others," he wrote. "When they are made to feel special and valued, children grow to respect themselves. A positive sense of one's self allows the maturing child to respect others."

As we have said previously in this book, self-respect is at the heart of respecting others. "When you can identify and appreciate your strengths and accept your vulnerabilities, it's easier to truly respect the value in others," Perry said.

Not surprisingly, what a child respects is determined by a large part to what they are exposed to. "Young children begin to respect things they see in the adults who are present in their lives, both good and bad," Perry said. "Let children see how you show respect for all people, including the elderly, authority figures such as police officers, and people who are different from you in terms of ethnicity or religion."

Viewed this way, we can see that teaching respect to children does not fall to parents alone. Other family members, such as grandparents, aunts, and uncles, and people in the community, such as teachers, religious leaders, even neighbors, share a responsibility, and through their modeling of what respect looks like, they can positively influence younger generations.

Asheesh Advani, the CEO of Junior Achievement Worldwide, described in an essay titled "Silver Linings"[15] published in *Work Is Love Made Visible* a practice within his family that teaches the children gratitude. Regularly, they tell each other three things for which they are thankful that day. The first one or two generally are easy enough to come up with: a good test score, a favorite dessert after dinner. But finding a third one often becomes harder and "nudges the mind to turn otherwise negative experiences into positive ones, for example, missing the school bus, but still getting a ride to school."

"The mind starts to develop the habit of looking for the positive in everything," he said. Gratitude for what they have breeds optimism.

Optimism, I believe, is fertile ground for respectfulness to take root.

■ ■ ■

We've talked a lot about infusing respectfulness into your personal relationships with friends, family, a spouse, and modeling it for children. The benefits are many:

- ◆ There is less drama over disagreements and more understanding, perhaps even collaboration.

- Your friends, family, and colleagues feel valued by you. Children learn respectfulness from you.
- You boost your self-confidence as you act authentically. You feel good!

My son Geoffrey said to me the other day, "I believe this family is everything." His perspective is enriched by being a father. And he's right. Everything begins and ends with the family.

Think About It

1. What is it you see when you look out the window that is visible but not yet seen by others?
2. The next time you disagree with someone, pay close attention to the words you use. Do they make your point or escalate the situation?
3. How will you model respectfulness to the children in your life?

CHAPTER 8

Respectfulness in Civic Institutions

There is a story behind every person. There is a reason why they are the way they are. Think about that, and respect them for who they are.
— Ziad K. Abdelnour

For Dr. Miguel Cardona the Golden Rule comes to mind when considering how to infuse everyday interactions with respectfulness, whether it is in the classroom or in the community. "It's basic; just treat people the way you want to be treated," he said. "No matter where I am, it's something that I've tried to do. If I'm in my office and the person who cleans my bathroom walks in, I want to treat that person with the same level of respectfulness as when I'm standing in the Oval Office and the president walks in."

That scenario is not hypothetical for Cardona. As the country's Secretary of Education during the Biden administration, he has been in the Oval Office many times. Though a cabinet-level position is a high honor, the greatest influence on the way Cardona treats others comes from his hard-working parents and the close-knit family community in which he grew up. That is still important to him.

"To me, it's bigger than any one person or title, it's just humanity, right? Treat people like we're all the same. Titles or letters after your name don't matter."

Miguel Cardona began his career in education as a fourth-grade teacher in the small-sized city of Meriden, Connecticut, where he grew up. Within a few years he was named principal of another elementary school in the city, becoming at 28 the youngest public school principal in the state's history.

Following positions of increasing responsibility in education, he was appointed Connecticut's Commissioner of Education, guiding it through the early years of the pandemic with concern for the effects of long-distance learning on students' mental health. He reached a pinnacle of American public education when he was sworn in as the 12th Secretary of Education for the country in 2021 and served until 2025.

In that role of responsibility for the nation's 65 million students, he led efforts to transform the country's student loan system, which resulted in greater accountability in higher education and more than $185 billion in debt relief to almost five million Americans. Under his leadership, the United States saw the greatest one-year growth in reading achievement for lower performing students since 2009.

Dr. Cardona was a graduate of the high school vocational-technical system in the automotive studies program. He received a bachelor of science degree in education from Central Connecticut State University followed by a master's degree, sixth-year certificate, and eventually his doctorate in education from the University of Connecticut.

He was a first-generation college graduate who celebrates bilingualism and biculturalism as a superpower. Among his awards are the Outstanding Administrator Award from the University of Connecticut's NEAG School of Education and in 2012 the National Distinguished Principal Award for the state of Connecticut.

His parents moved to Connecticut from Puerto Rico—his mother came as a youngster with her five siblings when her mother, who had cancer, needed health care. Spanish was Cardona's first language; he learned English in kindergarten.

"For as long as I can remember, our home was always a place where people came when they needed a meal or someone to talk to, when they needed to be lifted. It was the hub of our family.

"I always say I was born rich, but I didn't have material possessions," Cardona said. "So I had what I needed, and there was that upbringing of respectfulness and service to others that allowed me to advise the president."

His father was a police officer and also served the community as a director on various boards; his mother worked in factories, mostly. Together they modeled community service so well that all three of their children entered public service: one son became a police lieutenant, a daughter was a school social worker, and Miguel Cardona, as we know, went into education.

In this chapter, we will see how he and other leaders developed respectfulness in schools. We will explore respectfulness in politics, that thorniest of public areas, and how to revive it in civic life. We will look at how respectfulness can be possible among fervently held religious differences.

As individuals, we can bring an attitude of respectfulness to every facet of our lives. We've seen how to do so in the workplace, in Chapter 6. We've seen how to do that within families and personal relationships in Chapter 7. It is our institutions that codify virtues, such as respectfulness—or at least they should.

Let us begin with education. "First of all, you model it," Cardona said. "You've heard that it doesn't matter what you say, it's what you do. And that doesn't mean you can't be honest about struggles that you're having or a challenge that you're having.

"But if you tell them to be respectful and then they see you raising your voice at a student or talking negatively about a colleague of yours in front of the students, then you're not modeling respectful behavior."

I would say that such modeling is also pertinent to leading in the workplace or raising your children and grandchildren. In a classroom, you also have to come up with shared values but must be careful to not put your values on the kids. Shared values are called *norms* in education.

"I didn't give them to the kids," Cardona said of norms, "I said, 'We're going to develop what we expect when we're together.'"

Examples would be actions such as raising your hand when you want to speak. Make sure you're being respectful of each other and use manners.

"So the students will come up with operating norms that they want to see from everyone and once you have these shared norms or values in the classroom, then when there's a breach and a student is admonished for it, it's not because I think you're a bad kid; it's because these are the norms that we agreed upon."

At the beginning of the school year, students sign the norms they developed. As the year progresses, some might be added, such as during recess everybody should be playing with somebody else, or we shouldn't be talking behind each other's back. In doing so, respectfulness is taught.

"To me, that approach matters because it requires compromise, it requires shared accountability, which is more important than when the teacher is watching because when the teacher turns his or her own back, all bets are off," Cardona said. "But if we agree that we're going to hold each other accountable, then they're more likely to be sustainable and they're more likely to be embedded in the students' natural way of doing business."

I like this approach for the responsibility it gives students to make their space—in this case, the classroom—fair and supportive. To use a psychology term, they have *agency*. Just think how such responsibility can carry over as they grow.

■ ■ ■

Stuart Muszynski's nonprofit foundation, Values-in-Action, provides similar programs for schools and communities across the country.

(See Chapter 2 for more detail.) Values-in-Action works by promoting kindness. "Kind people are respectful people," Muszynski said. "So if we get to kindness, we get to respect as a side benefit. That's the beginning point—something more organic."

The program encourages kids to pledge to Be Kind and Stick Together.[1]

The pledge includes the following:

- "Stop hurtful teasing and encourage others to do the same."
- "Do my part to make my school a safe place by being kinder to others."
- "Not let my words or actions hurt others."
- "Treat others the way I want to be treated."

The pledge, built on social-emotional learning, can be a potent counter to bullying in schools. "It tips the culture to a kindness environment," Muszynski said.

Since 2015, the Be Kind and Stick Together curriculum has reached more than 2.1 million students in all 50 states and four countries in more than 5,000 schools.[2] It's free. By the way, the "Stick Together" slogan is a nod to sponsorship by the company Duck Brand.

■ ■ ■

To go a step further in understanding why and how shared norms and pledges work, we can look to child psychologists, such Edward Deci and Richard Ryan, whose self-determination theory of motivation posited that children need a feeling of confidence and a sense of belonging. Actually, don't we all?

"I've seen examples where behaviors of bullying have led students to admonish other students, not because they were going to tell the teacher," Cardona said, "but because they have broken the code. There's a likelihood that if you continue to break that code, then you're not belonging to the group that created it. So there's an intrinsic motivation to be committed to the values. It's not extrinsic or compliance based. It's more like, I really want to be a part of this community because this community is great. It's bigger than me.

"It's bigger than just coming up with rules and having students agree to them. It's creating a sense of belonging to a community around respectfulness."

The concept is the same for leading an organization. You create a culture and probably you don't call it *norms* or have employees sign pledges. But the agreement is, for example, that you show up to work on time, you pull your own weight, you treat all with respectfulness. It is easier to lead when there's a culture of shared expectations and not just the boss saying so.

■ ■ ■

To explore the teaching of respectfulness in education, let's look at the first classroom for the nation's top educator and at his office now. Miguel Cardona was 23, fresh from graduating magna cum laude, when he was hired in 1998 as a fourth-grade teacher for an inner-city school. He set up his classroom with a bulletin board on the wall that said: "Let the Journey Begin!" above a rocket and 20 stars—one for each student.[3] A poster on another wall said, "You never know what you can do until you try."

With four clusters of five desks each, the classroom was arranged for cooperation among classmates, a cornerstone for developing respectfulness.

Fast-forward through a remarkable career that only 23 years later brought him to the highest education office in the land. Miguel Cardona personified the affirmation from the poster in his first classroom.

Now in private practice as an education consultant, his office bears a visual reminder of what is important to him. Behind his desk is a large, framed photo of fourth and fifth graders from an elementary school in Virginia. The students were visiting the Department of Education to sing during a conference.

"I went down and saw them perform and I said, 'Hey, do you want to check out my office?' I kind of disrupted the whole schedule.

We went into my conference room and just hung out and had small talk about 'What's working in schools? What do we need to fix? If you had a magic wand, what would you change?' It's always good to be around students."

Can you imagine how these 9- and 10-year-olds must have felt? They were asked for their opinion. They were treated as though they mattered. They received respect.

This likely was a life lesson they will never forget.

■ ■ ■

Team sports give children the chance to learn how to win without gloating, how to lose without blaming, and how to respect opposing team players as well as each other.

As a Little League coach for a team of 9- to 11-year-olds, Michael DeGarmo said he developed an acronym to help the baseball players learn and display respect: R.O.O.T.S.[4] Respect the rules. Respect the officials. Respect your opponents. Respect your teammates. Respect yourselves.

"Without rules chaos would ensue. The rules are designed to facilitate fair play, and they provide the boundaries for the game," DeGarmo wrote in a LinkedIn post. "Teaching kids to properly follow the rules teaches them to follow laws."

By respecting the officials in baseball, the umpires, children learn the value of authority, even if umpires might not get every call right. Children learn sportsmanship through respecting their opponents. They learn that the other kids want to play, win, and have fun, just like them.

One of the greatest ways this is done in youth baseball is by shaking hands with opposing team members at the end of the game, regardless of the outcome, DeGarmo noted.

Teammates have varying levels of abilities, but usually all want to get better at the game, which creates a common bond. Meanness, name-calling, or insults are forbidden; supporting each other is encouraged.

Young players can be hard on themselves when they strike out or miss a throw to third. A technique DeGarmo used when he saw kids knocking themselves over a mistake was "to laugh it off." The sooner kids realize that no one is perfect and we all make mistakes—but keep trying—the better.

"The key is how we react when we make those mistakes," he said. "Teaching a child to respect themselves encourages growth and positive self-esteem and goes a long way to helping them respect others with the same struggles."

Positive reinforcement of respect on and off the baseball diamond—or football and soccer fields or basketball courts or swimming pools or running tracks, you name it—can carry over into adulthood.

■ ■ ■

While the teaching and modeling of respectfulness is foundational in elementary schools, the importance of the virtue must be reinforced in middle and high school and beyond to the university level. In the early years of schooling, children learn the concept of respectfulness—how to define it and recognize it in behaviors. They are shown tools for developing self-respect, which we have noted in Chapter 4 is essential to authentically respecting others. And they are encouraged to engage with respect for others.

In the middle school years as children continue to grow into their identities, teachers—and parents—can offer tools, such as asking, "What are three things that you are good at, and how do you know?" The answers can be written or, for the artistically inclined, drawn, and then shared so classmates can learn about, and appreciate, each other.

This activity suggested by Mark Brown, a former middle school teacher, in his blog on activities for teaching respect in the classroom,[5] is particularly useful in schools, youth-oriented groups such as scouting or church, or at home. Answer the question "Who are you?" with four one-word answers. Everyone has different ways of identifying themselves, Brown said.

"For older students, discuss how society views these different identities. Are some perceived as 'good' or 'bad' and why is that so?" he said.

Universities, both private and public, have been criticized in recent years for either discouraging unpopular viewpoints, such as by canceling the appearance of ultra-conservatives, or by not tolerating campus protests on polarizing issues and world events.

It would seem that respect for each other's opinions stops when they run counter to yours. This is regrettable in an environment where of all places free speech must be encouraged not only as a Constitutional right, but also as a way to hone critical thinking.

As President John F. Kennedy wrote in his speech intended for delivery in Dallas, November 22, 1963, "Leadership and learning are indispensable to each other."[6]

Respectfulness in Politics

For some, respectful politics might sound like an oxymoron. The major parties denigrate each other, and bipartisanship, at least in Congress, is rare. A recent Pew Research Center survey showed that 65% of Americans polled said they always or often feel exhausted when thinking about politics.[7]

"Americans have long been critical of politicians and skeptical of the federal government. But today, Americans' views of politics and elected officials are unrelentingly negative," the Pew report stated.

"Majorities say the political process is dominated by special interests, flooded with campaign cash and mired in partisan warfare. Elected officials are widely viewed as self-serving and ineffective."

Such criticism was directed at both major political parties and all three branches of the federal government. But it hasn't always been that way.

Former Republican US Senator Phil Gramm of Texas said the atmosphere was different when he was in the Senate. He recalled being close friends with Senator Robert Byrd of West Virginia—a Democrat—in the years they served together.

"He certainly wanted more government than I did, and we fought over everything from the budget to line-item veto, but I had profound respect for him and he didn't want to tear the system up," Gramm said.

It is different now, he believes. "I do think there is a breakdown of respect in the protocol of the Senate, which is based on respecting other members. In debate today, people say things in the Senate that they would not have said before and couldn't have gotten away with saying.

"When Senator Byrd and I were there, we would have called out somebody for impugning the motives of somebody else. They don't do that now as much as we did then."

Phil Gramm is an economics specialist, author, and former politician. He was a professor of economics at Texas A&M University for 12 years before entering public service as a politician.

He was a Democrat first and then switched affiliation to the Republican Party. He represented the sixth District of Texas from 1979 to 1985, then was elected to the Senate where he served from 1985 to 2002.

Gramm is known for trying to reduce federal spending and as chairman of the Senate Banking Committee he worked toward modernizing banking, insurance, and securities laws.

He made a brief run for the presidency in 1996 but withdrew early in the primary process.

On leaving the Senate, Gramm was vice chairman of UBS Investment Bank, then a senior partner at US Policy Metrics, an economic and public policy research firm.

Phil Gramm is one of the smartest people, in terms of the economy and taxes, I know. He loves Texas, he's got Texas in his drawl, but he's a man who really cares about the United States and does whatever he possibly can to advance his views on the economy, taxes, and everything else. His op-eds on tariffs, in particular, frequently appear in the *Wall Street Journal.*

Gramm came to my house one time for dinner—we have these dinners of maybe 25 people—and I said "Senator, would you like to say anything to the group here?" and he stood up and said, "Well, I'm not really prepared" and he proceeded to talk for 15 or 20 minutes. He is very, very good at that.

Gramm has been a confidant of every president, going back through at least George H. W. Bush. He played that game in Washington for a long time. He knows where the slings and arrows are coming from and knows how to deflect them and do the right thing. It's a matter of respect.

Every human being deserves a certain amount of respect, Gramm said. "The quickest way for somebody to lose my respect is for them to be disrespectful in dealing with people who are far below them on the economic ladder. I go out of my way to be respectful of people; in part it's just good manners."

Above that basic level of respect which all humans are due, he said, is the respect that either people earn or that comes with a certain office they hold or a status they've attained.

"For example, I might not like a certain president. But I would never speak of them or to them or about them in a disrespectful manner. I knew Joe Biden well for 18 years, and I see him at funerals and fundraisers now, but I would never call him Joe," Gramm said months after Biden was out of office. "He was president of the United States and it's a title I will always call him by. I may disagree with him on many things, and I do. But that doesn't change the fact that he was president."

It would be good for society if more people saw respect, regardless of political party, in that light. Stuart Muszynski, of Values-in-Action, believes that the messaging in political leadership has to change and that change will begin with the public.

"Politicians who are rude and crude will say anything they need to in order to accomplish their goals," he said. "Everybody understands that. That's why there has to be a counterbalance and that is kindness. Politicians are not going to be leaders in this, but if society leads with kindness they will be fast followers."

Could there be a tipping point when the public will get involved again? Michael Dowling, CEO emeritus of Northwell Health, predicts that more people will be speaking up in support of democracy and free speech in the United States.

"People are living in fear right now, and I don't think they have yet figured out that the trend we're on is a very, very dangerous one. But I think that people will have to speak up and will be speaking up a lot more. I never thought that in the United States I'd be worried about being able to speak my mind, but that's the reality. And people have to understand that if it continues, we won't have the America that we believe we had."

When Michael Dowling and I spoke about respectfulness for this book, it was a time in this country when the federal government was pulling or withholding funding from independent institutions such as private universities, hospitals, museums, and even certain law firms.

"We can disagree on programs; we can disagree on strategy. That's legitimate. That's what democracy is about. But you shouldn't be undermining the values that are the key to who we supposedly are," Dowling said.

One of those bedrock values is free speech, guaranteed in the First Amendment to the US Constitution.

"Free speech is not about 'I will only agree with free speech as long as you agree with what I say,'" he said. "That means a lack of respect for points of view that are contrary to yours, a complete lack of respect."

MaryLou Pagano, executive director of The Sheen Center for Thought and Culture in Manhattan, reflected that when she went to college in Washington, DC, during the Reagan years, there were students who were Republicans and some were Democrats and "no one hated each other."

Now, "we live in this world where my opinion matters more than yours. That's ridiculous." She thinks it's possible, and desirable, to be able to "believe this and still believe that." In other words, respectfulness for each other's opinion is not an either–or proposition.

She's right, I believe, but it is not easy. "It requires self-esteem, self-control, sensitivity, tolerance, fairness, and generosity. And it applies both to stated opinions and to opinions that are left unspoken," wrote P. M. Forni in his book, *Choosing Civility*.[8] Forni was the cofounder of the John Hopkins Civility Project.

"Respecting others' opinions doesn't mean being untrue to our own," he wrote. "It simply requires us to recognize that others are entitled to look at the world differently."

Even in politics. Sol Trujillo said, in an interview with *Latino magazine*,[9] that less polarizing language and more pragmatic solutions are needed. "As I think about politics, I think about all the issues—trade, immigration, balancing budgets, thinking about how we create more revenue without being heavily taxed. These are all things that are important to me. So I engage," he said.

In politics, success is a function of people liking you; in business success is related to your ability to deliver results. "In politics, as in business, you can force change," he said. "I might sound simplistic, but I believe it's possible."

I agree. It's possible when based on respect. Three political leaders who embodied courage and decency come to mind. All were US senators whose actions, when needed, transcended political affiliation.

Margaret Chase Smith took on fellow Republican Joseph McCarthy in 1950 and exposed him for having no proof that the State Department was infiltrated by Communists at the time. The Declaration of Conscience she helped prepare stated, "It is high time we stopped being tools and victims of totalitarian techniques—techniques that, if continued here unchecked, will surely end what we have come to cherish as the American way of life."[10]

Daniel Patrick Moynihan was a great believer in government transparency; he advocated for a free and independent press as essential to democracy. Moynihan, a Democrat who was ambassador to India, then the United Nations before coming to the Senate, is attributed with famously saying, "Everyone is entitled to his own opinion, but not his own facts."[11]

John McCain, a Naval officer during the Vietnam War, endured torture as a prisoner of war by the North Vietnamese for five-and-a-half years. He refused an early release offered because his father was the admiral in charge of US forces; he would stay until all men captured before him were released. He later was respected in Congress for voting according to his conscience, not party. When he was the Republican candidate running against Barack Obama for the presidency in 2008, he corrected a supporter at a rally who called Obama an Arab. McCain told her she was wrong and that Obama—his opponent—was a fine man.

If you did not know or remember the political party affiliation of Chase Smith, Moynihan, and McCain, you would be hard-pressed to identify it. You can read more about them and others in my book *Character: Life Lessons in Courage, Integrity, and Leadership.*[12]

Phil Gramm thinks it would be helpful if both parties could agree before the next election to dramatically reduce the executive authority of the president. "The problem is, when the Democrats are in power, they don't want to give up any of the power, and the same for Republicans. I tried to get the Republican administration when I was chairman of the Banking Committee to rein in the power of the president to use the Defense Production Act, since it basically makes him a dictator. But this is true of both parties: they don't want the other party to have the power, but they're not willing to give it up themselves."

He refers back to the country's founders and the formulation of the US Constitution. "The purpose of the Constitution was to basically take all the things that mattered and set the system of rules that Congress or the president couldn't change. I think the system has become less stable, less respectful, and more dangerous."

As individuals with our own worldview and responsibilities, we have to consider how we deal with disrespect. And the higher you go in a profession, the greater the opportunity for disappointment as perhaps programs you try to institute are thwarted. Disrespect could be evident as others fail to separate the person from the idea.

Miguel Cardona has learned how to navigate through such situations. "When you maintain a level of calm and respect, despite being disrespected, it does get noticed and it might be difficult in the moment but I think in the long term there's more benefit to being respectful than there is to fighting fire with fire."

Disrespect can be shown through actions or words. Phil Gramm developed a thick skin against negativity after so many years in politics. "If somebody calls me an S.O.B., you know, I would say, 'Well, and what's your name, sir?' Probably that's the best put-down so it's never any matter what anybody says to you. Being disrespectful to them is never good policy, in my opinion."

Respectfulness in Religion

Historically, religion has been a great divider. Wars have been waged for the sake of religious differences. This is ironic given that respect in one form or another is central to the tenets of most of the world's major religions.

Closer to our time, remember the so-called War on Christmas? It was a term coined by conservatives such as Bill O'Reilly in the early 2000s as backlash to efforts to make the greeting "Merry Christmas" more secular by saying "Happy Holidays" or "Season's Greetings." In fact, people could say what they wanted. But instead of raising awareness about various religions, the issue fed the notion of political correctness.

Today tolerance seems to be in short supply. Antisemitism is on the rise, not only in the United States but also around the world. The first administration of President Donald J. Trump tried to ban

Muslims from entering the country. Sex abuse scandals rocked the Catholic Church, which was accused of covering up the misconduct of some priests.

Religion remains steady, however, as an influence in American lives. A Pew Research Center survey found that a third of respondents said they attend religious services at least once a month, a level that hasn't changed since 2020.[13] Similarly, 44% of adults said they pray at least once a day.

Pew's Religious Landscape Study and other center polling from 2023–2024 showed that Christianity as a share of the population after years of decline has been stable, and the rise of the religiously unaffiliated population has leveled off. At a glance, 62% of American adults surveyed in that time frame describe themselves as Christian (40% are Protestant, 19% Catholic, and 3% other denominations); 29% say they are religiously unaffiliated (5% atheist, 6% agnostic, and 19% "nothing in particular"), and 7% belong to religions other than Christianity (2% Jewish, and 1% each Muslim, Buddhist, or Hindu).

The percentages might surprise you; they are a snapshot in time. What can one person do to bring respectfulness to the realm of religious differences? At the basic outward level, have respectfulness when visiting houses of worship.

"If you walk into a Buddhist temple in China, you have to be respectful of the rules. If you walk into a synagogue, show respect and put on a skull cap. You go into a mosque, you remove your shoes; that is respectful," said Rabbi Arthur Schneier, a spiritual leader of the Park East Synagogue in Manhattan since 1962. He is a founder of the Appeal of Conscience Foundation. Learn more about Rabbi Schneier and his leadership on religious freedom, human rights, and tolerance in Chapter 9.

There are ways to engage with aspects of other religions without impinging on your personal beliefs. MaryLou Pagano, the executive director of The Sheen Center for Thought and Culture, believes that faith lends itself to finding commonality and countering the splintering of society. The center is affiliated with the Catholic Church.

"Cardinal [Timothy] Dolan says the center is the front porch of the Catholic Church," Pagano said. "If nothing else, people come in and are respectful of people who go into the church. Whether front porch or front pew, the arts is the place for mutual respect."

Many might think that religion is about services on a Saturday or Sunday in a place of worship, but actually religious beliefs influence many areas of life in the most personal ways. From the status of embryos derived from fertilization in a test tube to end-of-life autonomy for the terminally ill, people push their religious beliefs on others under the mantle of "right."

Religion is one of the most sensitive areas to navigate, even though respectfulness is codified in many. In the Ten Commandments, followers are told, *Love thy neighbor as thyself.*

In Islam, respect is a core principle. *It is the responsibility of each individual to treat all of creation with respect, honor, and dignity.*

Hinduism teaches that the divine is equally present in all. *No one is superior, none inferior. All are brothers marching forward to prosperity.*

A hallmark of Buddhism is a respect for all people. It teaches the importance of showing people *the same respect you would a Buddha.*

The value to show respect is a key element to the Jewish worldview. *That which is hateful to you, do not do to another.*

All of these are related to what's known as the Golden Rule that extends back to ancient times. Isocrates, a Greek rhetorician (436–338 BCE), said, "Do not do to others that which angers you when they do it to you."

On permanent display at the United Nations in New York City is a poster showing how the Golden Rule is applied in sacred writings from 13 faith traditions.

In recognizing and acknowledging what peoples of all faiths, or no faiths, have in common we have a path toward treating all with respectfulness.

Think About It

1. How could you incorporate ways respectfulness is taught in the schools into your personal life?
2. Consider what it would take to return respect to national politics. Consider what steps you could take.
3. Make it a point to learn about religions different than your own, starting with a neighbor or colleague. What might you have in common?

CHAPTER 9

Transforming Society

Mutual respect is the foundation of genuine harmony.
— The Dalai Lama

It can feel like the world is broken. People are quick to attack each other over differences in beliefs or backgrounds. Divisions over politics are chasms so wide it seems they can never be bridged. Civility is out, respect is on life-support, and it's everybody for themselves. Or so it seems.

Does it have to stay this way? I say no. It is not too late to transform society, but it will require the thought and deliberate effort of each one of us.

Rabbi Arthur Schneier shows the way. He is a leader of the Park East Synagogue in Manhattan and established the Appeal to Conscience Foundation in 1965, a human rights interdenominational nonprofit. "Bound by our shared destiny to heal our wounded world, we must emerge as a united human family, seeking improvement by building peaceful co-existence and respect the other," states the mission.[1]

Rabbi Schneier is, in my view, one of the most powerful rabbis in the United States. We have known each other for many years. He is a Holocaust survivor. "I lost my family at Auschwitz. I lived through the war thanks to the humanity of a Swiss diplomat. All these diplomats who risked their diplomatic careers in order to save lives shows respect for man's ability, women's ability, to rise. Respect is rising above division and hatred."

> As a young child living under Nazi occupation in Vienna and Hungary during World War II, Rabbi Arthur Schneier vowed that if he survived he would change the world into one of tolerance. Family members died in the Holocaust. Acting on his vow, Rabbi Schneier founded the Appeal of Conscience Foundation in 1965 and became internationally known for his leadership on behalf of religious freedom, human rights, and tolerance. He also is the senior leader of the historic landmark Park East Synagogue in Manhattan.
>
> Rabbi Arthur Schneier received the Presidential Citizens Medal from President Bill Clinton for "his service as an international envoy for four administrations and as a Holocaust survivor, devoting a lifetime to overcoming forces of hatred and intolerance" and Department of State Special Recognition Award for "his ecumenical work in favor of mutual understanding, tolerance and peace." The United States Senate honored him for his half-century of work on behalf of religious freedom and interreligious cooperation.
>
> Pope Francis conferred on Rabbi Arthur Schneier the rare papal knighthood of St. Sylvester for "his unceasing work to promote peace and mutual understanding."
>
> He has received 11 honorary doctorates from US and foreign universities. Among his many awards are the Nizmani Ganjavi International Award for "his role in fostering interreligious dialogue" and the Responsible Leadership Award for "A Lifetime of Achievement," Muslim World League.
>
> Rabbi Schneier is a member of the Council on Foreign Relations, Asia Society, U.S. Holocaust Memorial Museum Committee on Conscience, and a vice president of the World Jewish Congress. His alma mater, Yeshiva University, established the Rabbi Arthur Schneier Program for International Affairs.

Transforming Society

Every Holocaust Remembrance Day he gives thanks and honors the Swiss diplomats who rescued Jewish children from Nazi horrors.

But now, that value of respect that had risen "above division and hatred" decades ago is at risk. "We have seen, unfortunately, polarization throughout the world contribute to some of the vision that we have to counter," he said. "We're in the midst of major societal changes and technological changes and God created not only the good but also the bad. The command is—choose life.

"God gave you the blessing and the curse."

What does he mean by that, "The blessing and the curse"?

"Atomic energy was hailed and lauded for eliminating the consequences of coal, contamination, and pollution. But then you have the atomic bomb. And now you have AI, positive and negative. We are going through a major period of change. I think we'll be okay. And now wandering into the political situation, I pray for a *United States of America*."

He has seen, and unfortunately still does see, people's inhumanity to other people. "I say we have encountered the best of man and the beast of man," he said, coining a memorable phrase about the present times.

■ ■ ■

A hallmark of civility is respect for different views in the community, the workplace, in the executive suite, the boardroom, and in society generally. In fact, the voicing of a range of views should be encouraged to broaden each individual's perspective. True civility demands that we try to rise above subtle and not-so-subtle prejudices and help others understand the importance of respect and to recognize our common humanity.

In this book you have been given the opportunity to explore the many aspects of respectfulness—why it is needed now and a counterpoint debate on whether it truly can exist. We have looked at the philosophical and psychological underpinnings of respectfulness.

The map of action begins with strengthening self-respect, with steps on how to do it and how to avoid going overboard into the realm of narcissism. We have examined the lessons and possibilities of respectfulness in the workplace, family and personal relationships, and civic institutions such as education, politics, and religion.

Thirteen leaders in various fields have shared their insights about respectfulness and their experiences of dealing with disrespect. You will find this compendium nowhere else. Consider it a master class in respectfulness.

Society is hurting right now. Respect for fellow human beings appears low while ostracizing the "other" is high and in control. In this chapter we will delve into strategies "ordinary" people can take to revive a culture of respectfulness. By "ordinary" I mean every-day citizens; we don't have to wait to elect political leaders to do the work. You are hereby empowered.

■ ■ ■

Michael Dowling, the CEO emeritus of Northwell Health, has been speaking by invitation at conferences and seminars lately about the necessity of common values, such as decency, trust, and respect. "I think you're going to see more and more people speak up. I've been speaking up a little bit, but I'm going to have to do a lot more of it. But with the political environment we're in, you also have to pick your spots. You don't want to do something stupid and have the reaction be so bad that you would damage your own organization."

It's a balance, free speech with a dose of political reality. Sadly, we have seen leaders of universities and industries reluctant to speak out under the threat of federal funding getting withdrawn.

Dowling believes that people are longing for a return to values. He tells of the reactions to an acceptance speech he delivered recently. He was given an award by the Center for Economic Development in New York City, a group of high-powered CEOs, as he describes them, and mostly conservative. He was the last of five on the roster to receive the award and it was 9 p.m., when it can be expected the audience is ready to wrap things up. Other awardees talked about their shareholder value, balance sheets, and market shares; he decided to forgo his notes and go in a different direction.

"I said to them, 'I'm involved in the health care field and we run hospitals and medical centers, we have doctors and we have nurses and we have researchers, etc. But I want to expand the definition of health. What we need to be doing is promoting decency, respect, honesty, trust, and integrity and that leads to improved health.

"'And health is about how we deal with one another, how we talk to one another. How we respect one another's opinions. All of that improves health.'

"And what was amazing, people jumped to their feet and gave a standing ovation!"

The applause wasn't necessarily for his delivery, he said modestly. The positive reaction taught him something.

"Here you had an audience that would definitely be voting in a different way than I would vote but were very responsive to the understanding of my message." Values matter. Values are to be encouraged.

I believe that for a society to run smoothly we must have some shared values. But where can we find agreement? For some, honesty might be a given, whereas another group might place loyalty higher. Can we agree on integrity? Compassion?

Even the motto on the back of US paper money—In God We Trust—may not be a statement to which all would agree. If universal societal values are lacking, then individuals might look for common values within groups representing similar interests, such as political parties, nonprofits, and religious and community organizations. And this can be fulfilling to the extent that other-minded groups are not considered less—fill in the blank—smart, committed, pious, altruistic, and so on.

Personal values, those that are of topmost importance to you, can guide you when choices arise, decisions must be made, problems solved. They form a bedrock in relationships.

"You cannot impose your particular values," said Rabbi Schneier. "You must have respect for the difference of others."

Mitzi Perdue, who started a crowdfunding effort to clear land mines from Ukraine, is inspired by Mother Teresa's saying, "The good that we can do, we must do." She likes to ask people what their visions of the ideal world would be. The answers reflect a wide variety.

For some, it's no more war; for others, it's education for everyone or health care for all, maybe better stewardship of the environment. For some, it's more personal, such as getting to be the best parent they can be.

"It matters, because your answer will reveal a lot about what you value, and in the process, your answer will also reveal information about who you really are. What you care about is a window into your character," according to Perdue.[2] Let your window be clear.

Standing up for others is a value that translates from the playground to the world stage. "It takes a lot of courage, a lot of love, to stand up and say something. To communicate in such a way that the words I am using are not demeaning, degrading, or resort to name-calling," said Sarah McArthur, editor in chief of *Leader to Leader*, the quarterly journal of the Frances Hesselbein Leadership Forum. She had witnessed Hesselbein, the CEO of the Girl Scouts at a pivotal time for the organization, stand up for her values and others in a memorable way. (See Chapter 7.)

Rabbi Schneier describes the challenge of remaining respectful when encountering an injustice. You must stand up for those who are treated unjustly, no question. "In my experience during the military rule in Argentina when young men and women were disappearing because they were accused of being Socialists, I met with the president at the time.

"In order to defend their hostility, they called in the Minister of the Interior and the man was just lying and it took a lot of self-control on my part and my members of the delegation to not lash out. The president sensed our disgust so he didn't push the point any further.

"I spoke to him about crying mothers, two Catholic, one Protestant, and one Jewish, whose young children, in their 20s, university students, just disappeared. They were dropped from helicopters into the ocean. I asked the president 'Who did it?' and he said he didn't know. But if he knew, he said, 'Can you certify that?' These are encounters where human dignity is compromised.

"Argentina today is a different country. This lesson leads me to conclude that every conflict comes to an end," Rabbi Schneier said. "And we need above all to make sure we save human lives."

Stand up for those who cannot. Put your personal values into action.

■ ■ ■

The devolving of civil discourse has been blamed on the proliferation of social media and the blame is warranted. The internet has been, as Rabbi Schneier ascribes to other key developments, both a blessing and a curse. A wealth of information is at the fingertips of anyone with a computer and a wireless connection. It's mind-boggling to think that information once was promulgated by monks painstakingly putting words on parchment centuries ago—and available only to certain classes. Fast-forward to mere decades ago when anyone could walk into a public library and thumb through hand-typed index cards for instructions on where to find a particular book or periodical. Kids today might laugh at that, akin to using a manual typewriter where you have to move a lever left-to-right at the end of every sentence! And now, you don't even have to leave your home or search for a book—it's all right there on your laptop. Within seconds.

A downside, however, is that it takes effort, and maybe some savvy, to sift through the deluge of information to find original sources, to get close to the truth. Companies pay for search engine optimization—to have links to their sites at the top of a search. How can you decipher what is reputable? And annoyingly, it's easy to inadvertently land on an advertisement promoting some wonder drug supplement or another.

What I've been describing is accessing information. When we talk about social media we mean engaging with the information—commenting on news stories, for example—or communicating with others in posts, messages, reels, and videos.

Social media has come to be a broad term. In its simplest definition, it is an internet-based form of communication.

We recognize it as person-to-person photo and message sharing sites, such as Facebook, X (formerly known as Twitter), Instagram, and others. There are primarily video platforms, such as YouTube and TikTok. Enter the rise of influencers.

This is not to say that all social media is evil and should not be used. Some is beneficial, some is harmless. But it ought not to be like a lawless Wild West where justice is a matter interpreted by the boldest and anything goes.

Of course, some of this is helpful community building, such as providing reminders to wish a happy birthday to a classmate you haven't seen in decades. But some is psychologically damaging, especially to children.

Reel after reel of friends out with other friends, wearing the latest of-the-moment fashion, and seeming to have fun, can erode the self-confidence of young people. There have been Congressional hearings on suicides related to competitiveness and also bullying on popular internet sites.

"There is a direct correlation between the addiction to social media and the pressure and anxiety and suicide," noted health leader Dowling. "I don't use social media that much and I think I benefit from the fact that I don't. I mean, I don't want to be hearing about what some idiots are talking about and just want to make news. Negative, negative, negative all the time and that's not good."

He is hoping to conduct a forum in New York City on the ill effects of social media on health. "We're seeing the results of it in our facilities," he said. "We have a major program right now which is packed to the gills focused on preventing college kids from committing suicide. The levels of suicide have accelerated and the question is why?

"People just don't want to deal with the world. What's happening is negative. So for me, it's an overall community health issue."

Social media affords in some places anonymity so people are more likely to post comments they would never say to someone's face. "Social media has benefits, but it has that other disastrous side to it," Dowling said. "In many ways it's a modem for communication for cowards who don't want to put their name on anything but just put garbage out there and get people to follow it."

Falsehoods get circulated and after a while they sound like the truth. "In the digital era, there are no bounds," observed international business executive Sol Trujillo.

And that is so. Denigrations and insults get liked and reposted to the point it looks like a majority feels the same way. You see how easy—and dangerous—it is to manipulate public discourse and thereby public opinion.

"Social media has destroyed things," said former corporate executive Indra Nooyi. "You can be disrespectful on social media anonymously; it's given you a license to do that. Because there's no name and face to it, you can say whatever you want and then just erase it or restate it in a different way. You can just play with it any which way you want."

The tone is set and condoned by the country's leaders, as has always been the way with other modes of communication from debates (think Lincoln-Douglas) to radio "fireside chats" to televised speeches. The internet, however, enables a speed and reach never before seen.

"Unfortunately, as leaders behave, so goes everybody else," Nooyi said. "And I'm already beginning to see disrespectful discourse in newspapers and television. So I think we are in uncharted territory. But who am I to say? Just because we're in that environment today, we should not assume that that's the way we should behave. We should figure out how to bring respect back into our society."

And there is the challenge. How can we bring respect back into our society? Let us look at language, the basis of communication from one person to another. In anonymous comments on social media sites, coarseness gets attention.

Would it help to rephrase the negative to positive? Psychologists H. Holloman and P. H. Yates believe so. They devised 11 categories of words that foster respect.[3] While aimed at classroom teachers, they are applicable to all. (See Chapter 5 for details.) An example: use words of unity that will foster a culture of collaboration and cooperation instead of the fallback "Because I told you so."

Closer to home, what are the words used to get a child to do the chores or a spouse to listen? Are the words accusing—"You never set the table without me telling you!"—or neutral—"Time to set the table!" The effect is cascading.

At least in the home or other personal settings, the tone carries the message of the words. But in digital communication, such as texts and emails, the nuance of tone is missing. The language becomes transmission instead of communication, notes podcaster and Texas attorney Jefferson Fisher in his book *The Next Conversation: Argue Less, Talk More*.[4]

"True connection involves sharing information with depth. It gives way for delivery and context. It touches your deepest needs to belonging, understanding and expression."

However, texts and emails are transactional, receiving signals through a cold medium. "Transmission is efficient, to be sure, but indifferent to understanding and authenticity," he said.

The problems are apparent. "It's the reason people write things in the comment section of social media apps that they'd never say to someone's face. It's why texts and emails can easily be misinterpreted. It's why people feel protected behind a keyboard. With transmission the human connection isn't there. ... You're meant to feel the warmth of a smile, not read it in an emoji," Fisher writes.

The human connection in language gets even further removed with the emergence of AI, aka artificial intelligence. Those in the publishing field may be among the first to see the consequences, along with professors reading student papers.

"With the rapid pace of technology brought on by technologies, self-publishing, now we've got this thing that creates stuff for us, so much information, content, communication coming at everybody at all times. It's definitely changing humanity as we know it; it's changing us," Sarah McArthur of the *Leader to Leader* journal told me. "This ability to so rapidly communicate that we don't even have to think about what we're saying. We can just turn and say, 'Give me 50 words to tell this guy where he can go with his ideas,' and we say, 'Oh, that looks good—send it!'"

No wonder disagreements can happen when people are relying on electronics to "talk" with each other. "It's our choice of words, how we articulate the message," said Sol Trujillo. "There's something good by being very direct, but that may come across as rude and make the other not willing to listen."

■ ■ ■

The COVID-19 pandemic that the country, and the world, endured may have dissipated, but effects continue to be felt and likely will for a long time. In schools, test scores confirm that students are behind in learning. In corporations and businesses, the shift is underway to end remote work and bring employees back to the office again. It is hardly seamless, though, as many employees had adjusted to the work-life balance allowed with working from home, such as walking the dog or taking a break to watch your child play sports, and were reluctant to go back to the time-consuming daily commute. On the flip-side, an untold number of places scaled back their office spaces and now don't have enough room for everyone to be there.

The social isolation felt during the pandemic has lingered. The restaurant industry reports that a sizable number of customers prefer to get take-out to eat at home rather than to sit at tables near others.

A disturbing trend adds to division: those who distrust the COVID vaccines and boosters versus those who consider them essential to public health. Both camps believe they are obviously right and the others are woefully wrong.

All of these pressures add stress and put civility to the test. For Cardona, it was important to never lose the human touch despite being on Zoom for work, which was a necessity during the pandemic and is still more commonly used now than before.

"When I would meet with folks whom I lead, I would always tell them that they have to prioritize their faith and sense of purpose. That's number one. Their health, their family, then work," he said of virtual meetings during the pandemic. "If they can take care of their faith, health, family, then they're going to be the best versions of themselves at work. In doing that, I'm showing respect to the things that they value.

"So before I start talking to you about whatever detail it is that I need you to do for work, I have to connect with you as a human. That's respectfulness and it gets a commitment and work productivity that's probably better than you would have gotten if you're just basing it on compliance and how well the mouse is moving."

Navigating education through pandemic, at the state, then federal level, was an unforeseen challenge with no ground plan.

With former US Surgeon General Vivek Murthy, Cardona visited schools across the country to make sure students' well-being was being addressed. "We were thinking about that, especially after the pandemic, so much so that he declared a youth mental health crisis in our country," Cardona said. "Basically, it's to say that we have to do more because the pandemic did create isolation so we had to double-down our efforts."

Society also has been torn apart and any sense of respect for fellow human beings ruptured with the epidemic of mass shootings in our country. The frequency is numbing. Not even a full four months into 2025, already 95 mass shootings had happened in the United States, with 125 killed and 374 wounded, according to the data collection site Mass Shooting Tracker.[5] On one day alone—April 13—mass shootings occurred in Daytona Beach, Florida; Conway, Arizona; and New Orleans, Louisiana.

No place is safe—not grocery stores, theaters, churches, synagogues, or schools.

Cardona went to Marjorie Stoneman Douglas High School in Parkland, Florida, where 17 students and educators were killed by a shooter in 2018. He went to Robb Elementary School in Uvalde, Texas, where 19 children and two educators were shot to death in 2022. He went to comfort and to seek answers.

"I visited different sites and talked to the parents and talked to the students. More often than not, it goes to a sense of belonging and a disconnect, I think."

The problem seems intractable for one person to resolve. But that is not a reason to turn a blind eye or accept mass shootings as a risk in life. Each of us has an obligation, I believe, to summon our values and address the root causes. A respect for human life requires action.

"We need to be a part of something bigger," Cardona said. "That's why it's so important to me to continue to uphold those American values of unity and belonging that I know are going to make our country continue to flourish despite the storms that may come."

Civics and Civility

Indra Nooyi, the former leader of PepsiCo, would like to see civics, including the notion of respect, to be taught in the schools. Teach students how to participate in government, what their roles and obligations are within a society.

"Civics goes with care for the country, care for the environment, respect for the people in your community," she said. "I think we have to go back to how important is civics? How do we teach it? How do we bring that whole notion of respect for everything around you back onto the front burner?"

Values need to be taught and reinforced. Parents have an obligation to instruct their children on the values that are important to them and the family—schools do not replace this. But not every child has the good fortune of such an upbringing; therefore, respectfulness for each other should be modeled and reinforced in the classroom.

Michael Dowling of Northwell Health shares Nooyi's viewpoint. "Schools have to rethink what they teach and that should be a real focus on how to teach kids about respectful behavior. How to teach kids about how to listen and understand and be less dependent on social media," he said.

"Schools have a huge responsibility here on how to live in a healthy community in a healthy way. And what is the sense of community? What does it mean? And teach people that we are all interdependent, you know nobody is successful by themselves. We all influence each other. The question is whether it's a positive influence or a negative influence."

Former Senator Phil Gramm considers civics lessons important as well. Youth need to have an understanding of how government works, the checks and balances, the history of political parties to be able to respect differing viewpoints.

"It's easier to compromise when you're not so far apart," he said. "Getting to know people is important. I find when I was in public life I spent more time around Democrats than Republicans do now. And I think that was helpful to them and to me."

The decline of civility must be reversed. Phil Gramm's approach of getting to know the other side instead of treating them as an enemy is a help in the right direction. Civility at its core means respecting the other person's point of view, no matter how wide of the mark, bizarre, or even ignorant you may think it is. You will rarely, if ever, convince adversaries to see things your way or moderate their position if you express contempt, disdain, or ridicule for an opposing point of view. That approach may score debating points, but it won't make a convert.

Don't question motives—discuss policies. Too many today take their cues from a polarizing, attack-oriented political culture. Help your adversaries understand they are as reasonable, thoughtful, and perhaps as smart as you are, but simply off-base on a particular issue, whatever it may be.

You can use responses such as "I understand why you hold that position. ... There may be merit in what you say. ... I respect your beliefs. ... Let's discuss an alternative."

Empathy, the ability to share in another's emotions, thoughts, or feelings, is the single quality that ensures one will act toward others with civility. In the classic novel *To Kill a Mockingbird*, Atticus Finch teaches his daughter Scout to be sure she sees things from the point of view of others. Express empathy by listening if someone wants to talk through a problem, speak a kind word, make a thoughtful gesture, such as showing up with a cup of coffee and a pastry. Show a generosity of spirit and you'll not only help someone else feel better but as a bonus you'll also feel better about yourself.

Despite your good intentions, disrespect will rear up. Someone will insult you and it will feel unfair; it will sting. But hold back on your immediate reaction to respond. Take a break, a few hours or maybe even a day, to think about what happened and why. Chances are you will forget about it and move on. This is a lesson that the late General Colin Powell told me about some years ago.

But if the insult deserves a response—and some certainly do, as you have to stand up for yourself—then the time you take for a break will enable you to formulate a constructive response instead of an emotional one in the moment.

Sometimes differences are so great they cannot be bridged. But they still can be respected. Phil Gramm admires Independent Senator Bernie Sanders's honesty, even though "I don't think there's a magic potion that we can put on that will eliminate the differences between Bernie and me unless he has a great awakening one night, which doesn't seem likely at this point."

Gramm told me this story. He was on an airplane a few years ago and across the aisle was Bernie Sanders. They had spent time in the Senate together; they recognized each other.

"I leaned over and said, you know, Bernie, I never agreed with you on anything, really, but I always admired the fact that you were honest."

"Some would try to say I'm nice, but he didn't," Gramm said. "I didn't react in any way. I just smiled and went on about my business." Both were being authentic.

Sarah McArthur, of *Leader to Leader*, reiterated that a big part of respect is listening but that can take effort when people are so impassioned about what they think. "It seems like today, more and more, the ears are closed. It's just this firehose of words."

Her strategy is to let them talk themselves out. "I'll listen until the person can hear themselves. I don't try to interject," she said. "Sometimes people are really self-aware and sometimes not. But they just want to be heard so I let them get it out."

Transforming

It is not too late, not a hopeless endeavor, to restore respectfulness for each other in American culture. MaryLou Pagano, of The Sheen Center, sees the arts as one pathway.

"Art is so healing. The arts are the place, whether it's a painting, a movie, a song. Art brings many people together. People want to laugh, to feel good about themselves," she said.

Bearing self-respect and acting with authenticity, people also can lift the atmosphere. "You can't change who you are and you shouldn't change, from the barrio to the briefing room," said education leader Miguel Cardona.

Despite the turmoil and divisions in society, many embrace an optimism for the future. Frances Hesselbein, the former Girl Scouts CEO, said every challenge is an opportunity. "In these times of great challenges, the opportunities are even greater for our new generation of values-based leaders. And it is the learning leaders who are the partners for ethical, principled, effective corporations and organizations. They will open doors," she wrote in an essay called "Be Positive!"[6] "We must shine a light in this age of cynicism. Our turbulent times cry out for leaders who live the mission, who embody the values, who keep the faith."

Could you be one of those leaders? Absolutely, by living your life with a sense of respectfulness for all. That light will spread. "Positivity begets positivity," MaryLou Pagano believes.

Research shows that people will respond to kindness with kindness, said Stuart Muszynski of the Values-in-Action Foundation. The foundation's programs are based on cognitive behavioral psychology, which establishes that the belief you put in your mind then establishes the resulting action. If the belief in your mind is kindness, then kind action will follow.

"All have the kindness gene and all have the meanness gene. It is up to us to make it come out," Muszynski said. "I haven't found anybody yet who doesn't have the kindness value, even if they do not express it."

As noted at the beginning of this book, treating others respectfully has life-changing consequences. It is the antidote to the inane, the meaningless, the disconnect of human interactions, the isolation.

We are social creatures and need each other, we need a sense of belonging to feel fulfilled. We must listen to what is said, and not said, listen to the beat of the human heart, which is the same for all no matter any differences.

You have the abilities now—and the power—to return respectfulness to its rightful place as a basic tenet of society. We can do better, and it begins with each of us. Let us start today.

Notes

Chapter 1: A Call for Respectfulness

1. "Malala's Nobel Is 'for all Girl Students of Pakistan,'" *USA Today*, October 10, 2014.
2. https://genius.com/Aretha-franklin-respect-lyrics
3. https://awaken.com/2022/01/quotes-by-margaret-mead/
4. Cheng Man-ch'ingá, *Lao Tzu: "My Words Are Very Easy to Understand": Lectures on the Tao Teh Ching*, Tam C. Gibbs (Translator). North Atlantic Books, 1993.
5. https://www.nytimes.com/2024/10/18/well/people-pleasing.html?smid=nytcore-ios-share&referringSource=articleShare
6. Sarah McArthur, Marshall Goldsmith, and Frances Hesselbein, *Work Is Love Made Visible*. John Wiley & Sons, 2019.
7. Hunter S. Thompson, *The Proud Highway: Saga of a Desperate Southern Gentleman 1955–1967*. Ballantine Books, 1997.
8. Michael Kardas, Amit Kumar, and Nicholas Epley, "Overly Shallow? Miscalibrated Expectations Create a Barrier to Deeper Conversation," *Journal of Personality and Social Psychology: Attitudes and Social Cognition*, 2021, *122*(3): 367–398.
9. Indra Nooyi, *My Life In Full*. Portfolio/Penguin, 2021.
10. https://www.facebook.com/100076134828159/posts/meryl-streep-i-have-no-patience-for-certain-things-anymore-not-because-i-have-be/6356364323
11. https://www.snopes.com/fact-check/to-patience-no-quarter/
12. Tom Junod, "My Friend Mister Rogers," *The Atlantic*, December 2019.
13. Vivek Murthy, "Social Media and Youth Mental Health," 2023. https://www.hhs.gov/sites/default/files/sg-youth-mental-health-social-media-advisory.pdf

14. Arthur C. Brooks, "Why Are Young People Everywhere Unhappy?," *The Atlantic*, May 1, 2025. https://www.theatlantic.com/ideas/archive/2025/05/young-people-global-unhappiness/682632/?utm_campaign=how-to-build-a-life&utm_content=20250501&utm_source=newsletter&utm_medium=email&utm_term=How+to+Build+a+Life
15. https://www.littleleague.org/university/articles/parent-guidelines-for-honoring-the-game/
16. https://www.popwarner.com/Default.aspx?tabid=2751349
17. https://kenburns.com/films/baseball-2/

Chapter 2: Is Respectfulness Truly Possible in the Age of Retribution?

1. https://www.viafdn.org/
2. https://stefanik.house.gov/2023/12/icymi-during-questions-from-stefanik-presidents-of-harvard-upenn-mit-refuse-to-condemn-calls-for-genocide-of-jews
3. Matthew Mpoke Bigg, "Pope Leo XIV Calls for News Media to Shun Divisive Language," *New York Times*, May 12, 2025.
4. https://www.oed.com/dictionary/respect_n?tl=true#:~:text=The%20earliest%20known%20use%20of,Etymons%3A%20Latin%20respectus
5. Edward N. Zalta and Uri Nodelman, *The Stanford Encyclopedia of Philosophy*. The Metaphysics Research Lab, Philosophy Department, Stanford University. https://plato.stanford.edu/
6. C. F. Cranor, "Kant's Respect-for-Persons Theories," *Journal of Value Inquiry*, 1982.
7. https://www.dilenschneider.com/files/civility_red_book.pdf
8. https://www.gutenberg.org/cache/epub/2680/pg2680-images.html
9. https://www.hhs.gov/sites/default/files/surgeon-general-social-connection-advisory.pdf
10. https://www.npr.org/2023/05/02/1173418268/loneliness-connection-mental-health-dementia-surgeon-general/

11. Sara Kettler, "Fred Rogers Took a Stand Against Racial Inequality When He Invited a Black Character to Join Him in a Pool." *Biography*, June 24, 2020. https://www.biography.com/actors/mister-rogers-officer-clemmons-pool
12. https://vtdigger.org/2018/12/25/officer-clemmons-carries-mr-rogers-message-hope/
13. A. O. Scott, "Review: Take the Next Trolley to 'Won't You Be My Neighbor?'" *New York Times*, June 6, 2018.
14. James H. Smith, "Opinion: The Day Mr. Rogers Silenced UConn Graduates," *The News-Times* (Danbury, Connecticut), December 7, 2019.

Chapter 3: What's in It for Me?

1. Kelly McKenzie, *Never, Never Hardly Ever*. Tolmie Press, 2024.
2. https://wordsworth-editions.com/book-author/sterne-laurence/
3. Matt Zajechowski, "Survey Reveals Most Americans Would Rather Sit in Silence than Make Small Talk," *Preply* blog, updated July 25, 2024, https://preply.com/en/blog/small-talk/
4. https://www.verywellmind.com/questions-to-engage-beyond-how-are-you-8699158#citation-2
5. https://www.gutenberg.org/files/885/885-h/885-h.htm
6. Allia Zobel Nolan, *101 Reasons Why a Cat Is Better Than a Man*. Adams Media Corp., 1994.
7. https://onlinelibrary.wiley.com

Chapter 4: Start with Self-Respect

1. Edward N. Zalta and Uri Nodelman (eds.), *The Stanford Encyclopedia of Philosophy*, September 10, 2003, substantial revision July 2, 2022. Stanford University.
2. Joan Didion, *On Self-Respect: Essay in Slouching Towards Bethlehem*. Farrar, Straus and Giroux, 1968.
3. David Brooks, *The Road to Character*. Random House, 2016.

4. https://www.ageist.com/ageist-podcast/being-deep-light-and-mindful-the-unflappable-alex-von-bidder/
5. https://podcasts.apple.com/us/podcast/being-deep-light-and-mindful-the-unflappable-alex/id1514482663?i=1000545832723
6. Robert L. Dilenschneider, *Character: Life Lessons in Courage, Integrity, and Leadership*. Citadel Press, 2025.
7. "The 500 Greatest Songs of All Time: Aretha Franklin 'Respect,'" *Rolling Stone*, 2021.
8. David Ritz, *Aretha: From These Roots*. Villard, 1999.
9. Ritz, *Aretha*.
10. Matt Minton, "Mel Robbins Extends Tour Dates," *Variety*, February 19, 2025.
11. Mel Robbins, *Let Them*. Hay House, 2024.
12. https://www.trustacrossamerica.com/blog/?p=2697
13. https://www.goodreads.com/quotes/9651823-just-believe-in-yourself-even-if-you-don-t-just-pretend

Chapter 5: The Top Five Qualities of Respectfulness

1. https://www.sheencenter.org/
2. Ibid.
3. Robert L. Dilenschneider, "Report: The Art of Listening." https://www.dilenschneider.com/reports.php
4. Jack Zenger and Joseph Folkman, "What Great Listeners Actually Do," *Harvard Business Review*, 2016.
5. Zenger and Folkman, "What Great Listeners Actually Do."
6. Buffalo Springfield, *For What It's Worth*, 1966.
7. David Brooks, "Voters to Elites: Do You See Me Now?" *New York Times*, 2024.
8. https://psychclassics.yorku.ca/Maslow/motivation.htm
9. Marilyn Price-Mitchell, "The Language of Respect: Walking Our Talk With Teenagers," *Psychology Today*, 2014.
10. David Brooks, *How to Know Others: The Art of Seeing Others Deeply and Being Deeply Seen*. Random House, 2023.

Chapter 6: Respectfulness at Work

1. Indra Nooyi, *My Life in Full: Work, Family, and Our Future*. Portfolio, 2021.
2. "Most Powerful Women of 2015 List," *Fortune*, 2015.
3. Frances Hesselbein, "My Journey with Peter Drucker," *Work Is Love Made Visible*. John Wiley & Sons, 2019.
4. Ibid.
5. Amy J. C. Cuddy, Matthew Kohut, and John Neffinger, "Connect, Then Lead," *Harvard Business Review*, 2013.
6. Amy J. C. Cuddy, Matthew Kohut, and John Neffinger, "Connect, Then Lead," *Harvard Business Review*, 2013.
7. Brené Brown, *Atlas of the Heart: Mapping Meaningful Connection and the Language of Human Experience*. Random House, 2021.
8. Cuddy, Kohut, and Neffinger, "Connect, Then Lead."
9. Sheryl Sandberg, *Lean In: Women, Work, and the Will to Lead*. Alfred A. Knopf, 2021.
10. Sheryl Sandberg, TEDWomen Talk. https://leanin.org/education/ted-talk-why-we-have-too-few-women-leaders
11. Ibid.
12. Robert I. Sutton, *The No Asshole Rule: Building a Civilized Workplace and Surviving One That Isn't*. Business Plus, 2007.
13. Robert I. Sutton, "Why I Wrote the No Asshole Rule," *Harvard Business Review*, 2007.

Chapter 7: Respectfulness in Family and Personal Relationships

1. https://www.hesselbeinforum.pitt.edu/publications/leader-leader-journal
2. Frances Hesselbein, Marshall Goldsmith, and Sarah McArthur, *Work Is Love Made Visible*. John Wiley & Sons, 2019.
3. Robert L. Dilenschneider, *The Ultimate Guide to Power & Influence: Everything You Need to Know*. Matt Holt/Ben Bella, 2023.
4. Hesselbein, Goldsmith, and McArthur, *Work Is Love Made Visible*.

5. Ibid., "Be Positive!"
6. https://www.oprahdaily.com/life/relationships-love/a64130885/how-to-start-tough-conversations/?utm_campaign=nlm01_032625_omc39166587&utm_medium=email&utm_source=nl_omc&utm_term=AAA+-+High+Minus+Dormant+and+90+Day+Openers+W%2F+Opted+In+Mylo
7. Julia Bozzone, "A Texas Lawyer Has the Words to Navigate Conflict," *New York Times*, March 23, 2025.
8. Jefferson Fisher, *The Next Conversation: Argue Less, Talk More*. Tarcherperigree Book, 2025.
9. Brené Brown, *Atlas of the Heart: Mapping Meaningful Connection and the Language of Human Experience*. Random House, 2021.
10. https://www.harvard.edu/in-focus/happiness/
11. Susan Dominus, "How Nearly a Century of Happiness Research Led to One Big Finding," *New York Times Magazine*, May 1, 2025.
12. Glenn Collins, "Children's Day at the Four Seasons," *New York Times*, August 24, 2010.
13. Alex von Bidder and Leslie McGuirk, *Wiggins Learns His Manners at the Four Seasons Restaurant*. Candlewick Press, 2009.
14. Bruce Duncan Perry, "Respect: The Sixth Core Strength," *Early Childhood Today*. https://teacher.scholastic.com/professional/bruceperry/respect.htm
15. Asheesh Advani, "Essay: Silver Linings," *Work Is Love Made Visible*. John Wiley & Sons, 2019.

Chapter 8: Respectfulness in Civic Institutions

1. https://www.viafdn.org/stick-together
2. https://www.viafdn.org/stick-together
3. Jacqueline Smith, "Songs of Innocence and Experience: No More Learning Factory, Says a Teacher of Today," *Record-Journal* (Meriden, Connecticut), August 30, 1998.
4. https://www.linkedin.com/pulse/teaching-kids-respect-through-baseball-michael-degarmo/

5. https://www.clickvieweducation.com/blog/teaching-ideas/respect-activities
6. https://www.jfklibrary.org/archives/other-resources/john-f-kennedy-speeches/dallas-tx-trade-mart-undelivered-19631122
7. https://www.pewresearch.org/politics/2023/09/19/americans-dismal-views-of-the-nations-politics/
8. P. M. Forni, *Choosing Civility: The Twenty-Five Rules of Considerate Conduct*. St. Martin's Press, 2002.
9. "Lessons of Leadership," *Latino*, Fall 2012.
10. https://www.senate.gov/artandhistory/history/resources/pdf/SmithDeclaration.pdf?utm_source=substack&utm_medium=email
11. https://www.vanityfair.com/news/2010/11/moynihan-letters-201011?srsltid=AfmBOoqNqJy-gIEkecHf961k9u
12. Robert L. Dilenschneider, *Character: Life Lessons in Courage, Integrity, and Leadership*. Citadel Press, 2025.
13. https://www.pewresearch.org/religion/2025/02/26/religious-landscape-study-executive-summary/

Chapter 9: Transforming Society

1. https://appealofconscience.org/
2. Mitzi Perdue, "Foreword." *Character: Life Lessons in Courage, Integrity, and Leadership*. Robert L. Dilenschneider (ed.). Citadel Press, 2025.
3. Marilyn Price-Mitchell, "The Language of Respect: Walking Our Talk with Teenagers," *Psychology Today*, 2014.
4. Jefferson Fisher, *The Next Conversation: Argue Less, Talk More*. Tarcherperigee, 2025.
5. https://massshootingtracker.site/data/?year=2025
6. Frances Hesselbein, "Be Positive!" Frances Hesselbein, Marshall Goldsmith, and Sarah McArthur, *Work Is Love Made Visible*. Wiley, 2018.

Acknowledgments

So many helped with this book.

I am greatly appreciative of the leaders who gave generously of their time to share their thoughts on the nature of respectfulness. They made the lessons come alive.

They are, in alphabetical order, Alex von Bidder, Miguel Cardona, Michael Dowling, Phil Gramm, Betsy McCaughey, Kelly McKenzie, Stuart Muszynski, Allia Zobel Nolan, Indra Nooyi, MaryLou Pagano, Sarah McArthur, Rabbi Arthur Schneier, and Sol Trujillo.

Sarah McArthur, editor-in-chief of *Leader to Leader*, provided the bridge to Wiley, and I am in her debt. If anyone understands respectfulness, it is Sarah, who learned it from the best, Frances Hesselbein, the founder of *Leader to Leader*. Frances was a positive influence in so many realms, and her inspirational work lives on, thanks to Sarah.

This book would not be possible without the thoughtful research of Jacqueline Smith and Robert Laird, whom I have worked with for many years. Each of them brings a unique talent to everything they do, and it is my pleasure to work with them. My colleague, Jonathan Dedmon, also made invaluable contributions. Working with him for nearly 40 years has been a privilege.

This book would not have been possible without my trusted assistant of many years, Joan Avagliano. Joan did everything from proofing to offering suggestions on content. She is here applauded.

Anthony Quiles-Roche, Yolanda Guzman, Keira Keelty, and Melanie Smith all provided strong support. I am grateful to Nataliya Lustig, Francine Benedetti, and Mirella DeMoura for keeping me on deadline. They are three of the best.

Jeanenne Ray, associate publisher at Wiley, recognized the need for this book to be published. I am indebted to the Wiley team of

Michelle Hacker, senior managing editor; Sherri-Anne Forde, editorial assistant; and Julie Kerr, who provided invaluable editing.

I am, as always, deeply grateful to my wife, Jan, who is in her own right a distinguished artist. She encouraged me to complete this, my 20th book, and offered insightful advice on the many points included here.

No acknowledgment would be complete without mentioning my supportive family: my sister, Martha, and her husband, Cort; my late brother and sister, Jack and Mary Lou Shay; my sons, Geoffrey and Peter, and their wives, Sabina and Julia; and my niece, Ricia Harding, along with husband, Paul, and their sons, Chase and Christian. I hope and believe our grandchildren, Bruce, Logan, Hailey, and Calvin, will study those in this book and shape their futures accordingly.

About the Author

Robert L. Dilenschneider formed The Dilenschneider Group in October 1991. Headquartered in New York and Chicago, the Firm provides strategic advice and counsel to Fortune 500 companies and leading families and individuals around the world, with experience in fields ranging from mergers and acquisitions and crisis communications to marketing, government affairs, and international media.

Prior to founding his own firm, Mr. Dilenschneider served as president and chief executive officer of Hill and Knowlton, Inc. from 1986 to 1991, tripling that Firm's revenues to nearly $200 million and delivering more than $30 million in profit. Mr. Dilenschneider was with that organization for nearly 25 years.

Mr. Dilenschneider started in public relations in 1967 in New York, shortly after receiving an MA in journalism from The Ohio State University, and a BA from the University of Notre Dame.

Experienced in a number of communications disciplines, Mr. Dilenschneider is frequently called upon by the media to provide commentary and strategic public relations insights on important news stories. He has counseled major corporations, professional groups, trade associations, and educational institutions, and has assisted clients in dealings with regulatory agencies, labor unions, and consumer groups, among others.

In 2001 he established The Borromean Lecture at St. Charles Preparatory School of Columbus, Ohio. The annual event attracts a nationally renowned speaker to talk on the topic of morals and ethics in business and government. In 2012 The Dilenschneider Group established the Civility in America Lecture Series, which features many of the nation's leading thinkers from a wide variety of professions and provides a perspective on what must be done to restore civility in our country.

Mr. Dilenschneider serves as a Trustee of the Institute of International Education and is a member of the North American Advisory Board of The Michael Smurfit School of University College Dublin. A member of the Ave Maria Law–Business Law Institute Advisory Board, he also serves as a member of the board of 54 Below.

He serves as a judge for The Olin Award, a program of the Olin School of Business at Washington University in St. Louis and is a member of the Council on Foreign Relations and the Economic Clubs of New York and Chicago.

Mr. Dilenschneider has also served on numerous corporate boards. A former member of the Board of Governors of the American Red Cross, Mr. Dilenschneider also served on the advisory board of the Center for Strategic and International Studies, the Board of Governors of the New York Chapter of the National Academy of Television Arts and Sciences, and The Bretton Woods Committee. He is a former member of the U.S.–Japan Business Council and the Florida Council of 100.

In 2001, he received an honorary Doctorate of Public Service degree from Muskingum College, and in 2012 he received an honorary Doctorate of Humane Letters from the University of New Haven. Mr. Dilenschneider is a Knight of Malta. He has been called the "Dean of American Public Relations Executives", and is widely published, having authored 19 books, including *Power & Influence, A Briefing for Leaders, On Power, The Critical 14 Years of Your Professional Life, Moses: C.E.O, The Critical 2nd Phase of Your Professional Life, 50 Plus!—Critical Career Decisions for the Rest of Your Life, A Time for Heroes, Power and Influence: The Rules Have Changed, The AMA Handbook of Public Relations, Decisions, Nailing It: How History's Awesome Twentysomethings Got It Together, the fifth edition of The Public Relations Handbook, and the Ultimate Guide to Power & Influence: Everything You Need to Know*. His most recent book, *Character: Life Lessons in Courage, Integrity and Leadership*, was published in 2025.

Mr. Dilenschneider has lectured before scores of professional organizations and colleges, including the University of Notre Dame, Ohio State University, New York University and The Harvard Business School.

Index

A
Abdelnour, Ziad K., 125
Accountability, 83, 126, 128
Active listening, 10, 48, 75–78, 94
Advani, Asheesh, 123
Agency, 16, 28, 97, 128
All Things Considered (radio program), 31
American Express, 103
American Psychological Association, 9
Anna Karenina (Tolstoy), 19
Appeal of Conscience Foundation, 4, 140, 144
Appreciation:
  of acknowledgment, 105
  and connection, 50
  in conversation, 77
  of differences, 94
  for elders, 80
  expressing, 105
  mutual, 132
  and respect, 83
  self-, 122
  of social effort, 48, 86
The Atlantic, 13–14
Atlas of the Heart (Brown), 99, 118
Attention:
  and authenticity, 98
  to children, 14
  example of, 43
  as form of respect, xi, 9, 27
  golden rules for, 114
  listening as, 74
  questions as, 122
  to quotations, 12
  to self, 61
  on social media, 1, 66, 152
  to speakers, 75–76
  to unspoken messages, 48
Attentiveness, 10, 77, 92, 97
Auburn Career Center, 22
Aurelius, Marcus, 30
Autonomy, 19, 28, 141

B
Bank of America, 92
Baseball (documentary series), 16
Belonging. *See also* Compassion
  Brené Brown's views on, 118–119
  in children, 129–130, 155
  and compassion, 7, 73, 81–82
  as connection, 152
  need for, 9–10, 159
  religious, 140
Biden, Joe, 125, 135
Biography (website), 33
body language, 10, 43, 94
Boeing, 109
Branson, Richard, 89
Breathing exercises, 46, 51, 114, 116
Brooks, Arthur C., 14
Brooks, David, 1, 58, 78, 85–86
Brown, Brené, 99–100, 118–119
Brown, Mark, 132
Burns, Ken, 16
Bush, George H. W., 135
Bush, George W., 91
Byrd, Robert, 133–134

173

Index

C

Cardona, Miguel, 3, 11, 50, 79, 85, 117, 125–130, 139, 154–155, 158
Castro, Fidel, 79
Center for Economic Development, 146
Character, 19, 26, 33, 52, 56, 58, 112, 148. *See also* Self-respect
Character (Dilenschneider), 61, 138
Chenault, Ken, 103
Chenoweth, Kristin, 72
Chesterfield, Lord, 44
Choosing Civility (Forni), 137
Church of St. Raymond's, 72
Citizenship, 107
Civic institutions, 5, 71, 125–142, 146
Civics, 155–158
Civil Rights Act, 33
Civility:
   and arguments, 115
   and civics, 155–158
   definition of, 29
   erosion of, xii
   and kindness, 21
   lack of reward for, 25
   long view of, 11
   in politics, 143
   as respect for different views, 145
   and social isolation, 153
   and social media, 149
   on television, 22–23
Clinton, Bill, 58, 91–92, 111, 144
Coaching for Leadership (McArthur), 108
Columbia University, 23
Columbus Citizen, 59
Compassion, 7, 68, 73, 81–82. *See also* Belonging
Compelling People (Cuddy, et. al.), 97
Confucius, 53
Connecticut Department of Economic and Community Development, 90
Connecticut Economic Resource Center, 90
Cornell University, 40
Cousins, Norman, 5–6
COVID-19 pandemic, 31, 43, 55–56, 153
Cuddy, Amy J. C., 97
Culture of connection, 32
Cuomo, Mario, 25, 55
Curiosity, xii, 48

D

Dalai Lama, 143
Dare to Lead (podcast), 99
Deci, Edward, 129
DeGarmo, Michael, 131–132
Deliberance, 116–117
Didion, Joan, 54
Dignity, 27–28, 54, 141
Dignity of human life, 7, 84–85, 107–108, 149
Dilenschneider, S. J., 59–60
Disagreement:
   and deliberance, 116–117
   digital, 153
   and disrespect, 114, 118
   in politics, 135–136
   respectful, 29, 79
   in sports, 15
   in workplace, 114–115
Disrespect:
   and bullying, 38
   as cause of conflict, xi, 2, 78
   and disagreement, 114
   towards leaders, 118
   and listening, 73, 99
   towards poor people, 55, 135
   recognizing, 71
   responding to, 26, 29, 86, 117, 157
   and self-respect, 64

Index

on social media, 30, 151
in workplaces, 3, 65, 91, 95–96, 101, 103, 139
Doby, Larry, 16
Dolan, Timothy, 141
Dole, Bob, 58
Dominus, Susan, 120
Doubleday, 42
Dowling, Michael, 3, 15, 54–57, 63, 65, 94–95, 104, 136, 146, 150–151, 155
Drucker, Peter, 3, 93–94, 108
Duck Brand, 129

E
Early Childhood Today, 122
Elizabeth Seton Children's, 72
Empathy, 83, 99–100, 156–157
Encouragement:
 and active listening, 77
 for children, 131–133
 of kindness, 20, 22
 program for, 129
 of respectfulness, 29
 self-, 67
 from social media, 63, 68
 of social skills, 14
 for teenagers, 82
 of values, 147
 in workplace, 104
Engagement:
 with children, 132
 for connection, 9–10
 with eyes, 76, 93
 in gossip, 105
 and lack of social connection, 31
 in opposite viewpoints, 80
 and religion, 140
 with screens, 30
 in small talk, 45
 with social media, 63, 150
Epley, Nicholas, 9
Expectations, 46, 71, 83, 91, 130

F
Fisher, Jefferson, 8, 114–115, 152
Folkman, Joseph, 77
Ford Motor Company, 109
Fordham University, 55, 57
Forni, P. M., 137
Fortune Magazine, 90, 111
Four Seasons restaurant, 3, 6, 39–42, 59, 110–111, 121–122
The Four Seasons (von Bidder), 39
F&R Lazarus & Company, 60
Frances Hesselbein Leadership Forum, 3, 108, 111, 148
Francis, Pope, 144
Franklin, Aretha, 5, 62
From Loyalist to Founding Father (McCaughey), 23
From These Roots (Ritz), 62
"Funny Girl" (musical), 119

G
Gandhi, Mahatma, 67
Gannett, 92
Gay, Claudine, 24
Gen Zers, 45, 63
Gender issues, 101–103
George Washington University, 109
Girl Scouts, 3, 8, 93, 110, 148, 158
Golden Rule, 21, 29, 125, 141
Goldsmith, Marshall, 108–109
Grace, 4, 16, 83
Graceful exits, 46–47
Gramm, Phil, 3, 25, 58, 64, 112–114, 133–135, 138, 139, 156, 157
Gratitude, 9, 32, 77, 79, 121, 123

H
Hanks, Tom, 13, 33
Harvard Business Review, 77, 96, 104
Harvard Business School, 97
Harvard Medical School, 120
Harvard School of Public Health, 55
Harvard University, 24, 55

Hearst Corporation, xii
Heavenly Headbutts (Nolan), 84
Hesselbein, Frances, 3, 8, 93, 107–108, 110–112, 118, 148, 158
Hinduja, S. P., 61
Holloman, H., 152
Holocaust Remembrance Day, 145
"Honoring the game" concept, 15
Hope, 83
How to Know a Person (Brooks), 85
Hudson Institute, 23

I
Instagram, 63, 114, 150
Integrity:
  as basic skill, 16, 22
  learning about, 59–60
  promoting, 147
  as value, 68
  verbal, 118
Iona Preparatory School, 72
Isocrates, 141

J
Jobs, Steve, 63
John Hopkins Civility Project, 137
Johnson, Philip, 39
Johnson Institute for Responsible Leadership, 108
Jones, Nora, 72
Judgment, 45, 46, 76–77, 97, 101–102
Junior Achievement Worldwide, 123

K
Kant, Immanuel, 27–29, 54, 63, 85
Kardas, Michael, 9
Kennedy, John F., 42, 133
Kettler, Sara, 33
King, Larry, 71
King, Martin Luther Jr., 33
Kohut, Matthew, 97
Kumar, Amit, 9

L
Lamont, Ned, 90
Latino Magazine, 137
Laugh Out Loud (Nolan), 84
Lazarus, Fred Jr., 60
Leader to Leader, 3, 8, 26, 51, 108, 110, 148, 153, 157
Leading Through a Pandemic (Dowling), 55
Lean In (Sandberg), 102
Leo, Pope, 26
Let Them (Robbins), 64
Letters to His Son (Chesterfield), 44
Loneliness, 8, 30–33, 66. *See also* Social isolation
Loyalty, 59, 94, 107, 147
Lurie, Saba Harouni, 48

M
McArthur, Sarah, 3, 8, 26, 29, 107–112, 116, 118, 148, 153, 157
McCain, John, 138
McCarthy, Joseph, 137
McCaughey, Betsy, 3, 11, 22–23, 25, 117
McGuirk, Leslie, 122
Machiavelli, Niccolò, 97
McKenzie, Kelly, 4, 37–38, 50, 77, 80, 103
Macy's Inc., 60
Mama Wicks, 111–112
Manhattan Institute, 23
Manners:
  in business, 41
  in children, 121, 128
  cultural variations of, 6
  external nature of, 43
  and respectfulness, 71
  social, 48–50
Marathon Oil, 10
Marjorie Stoneman Douglas High School, 155
Marshall Goldsmith, Inc., 109

Maslow, Abraham, 81–82
Maslow's hierarchy of needs, 81
Mass Shooting Tracker, 154
Mead, Margaret, 6
Meta, 102
Middling conversations, 44
Millennials, 63
Mindfulness, 10, 51–52, 59, 75, 92
Mister Rogers Neighborhood (television program), 33
Monroe, Marilyn, 42
Mother Teresa, 148
Mt. St. Michael's School, 72
Moynihan, Daniel Patrick, 137–138
Mulally, Alan, 109
Murthy, Vivek, 13, 30–32, 154
Muszynski, Stuart, 4, 19–22, 34, 125, 158–159
Muszynski, Susan, 4, 19
My Life in Full (Nooyi), 89

N
Narcissism, 146
Narrative takeover, 99
National Cyberbully Day, 20
Neffinger, John, 97
Never, Never Hardly Ever (McKenzie), 38
New Republic, 23
New York Mankind Project, 40
New York Post, 23, 24
New York Times, 23, 34, 78, 84, 108, 114, 120–121
New York University, 40
Newsmax, 22
The Next Conversation (Fisher), 8, 114, 152
The No Asshole Rule (Sutton), 104
Nolan, Allia Zobel, 4, 7, 50, 67, 84
Nonjudgmental attitude, 48
Nooyi, Indra, 4, 10–11, 16, 65–66, 76, 89–90, 95, 101–103, 106, 120–121, 151, 155

Norms, 93, 128–130. *See also* Standards
Northwell Health, 3, 15, 25, 55–56, 94–95, 136, 146, 155

O
Obama, Barack, 138
Onassis, Jacqueline Kennedy, 3, 42
100 Coaches, 109
Oprah Daily (electronic newsletter), 114
Optimism, 17, 56, 109, 123, 158
O'Reilly, Bill, 139
Oxford English Dictionary (OED), 27, 44

P
Pagano, MaryLou, 4, 71–73, 80, 86, 138, 140–141, 158
Paine, Thomas, 78
Park East Synagogue, 4, 140, 143, 144
Pataki, George, 3, 23
Patience, 77, 122
PepsiCo, 4, 11, 16, 65, 76, 89–92, 120, 155
Perdue, Mitzi, 148
Perry, Bruce Duncan, 122–123
Personal values, 52, 147, 149
Peter F. Drucker Foundation for Nonprofit Management, 108, 110
Pew Research Center, 133, 140
Physical stances, 100
Picasso, Pablo, 39
Politeness, 45, 48, 71, 122
Pop Warner Football, 15
Positivity, 46, 95, 158
Powell, Colin, 157
Price-Mitchell, Marilyn, 82
Priority, 14, 91–92, 97, 154
Project Love, 20
Psychology Today, 82

R

Redding, Otis, 62
Reese, Pee Wee, 16
Religion, 4, 82, 123, 139–141, 146
Religious differences, 127, 139–140
Remember the Children Foundation, 20
Reputation, 5, 23, 30, 67–68, 111
"Respect" (song), 62
Ritz, David, 62
The Road to Character (Brooks), 58
Robb Elementary School, 155
Robbins, Mel, 64–65
Robinson, Frankie, 37, 80, 103
Robinson, Jackie, 16, 107
Rogers, Carl, 75
Rogers, Fred, 13, 33
Rolling Stone, 62
R.O.O.T.S., 15, 131
Ryan, Richard, 129

S

Sandberg, Sheryl, 102
Sanders, Bernie, 157
Saturday Review, 5
Schneier, Arthur, 4, 79, 140, 143–144, 148–149
Scott, A. O., 34
Searching for Values (Muszynski), 20
Self-determination theory of motivation, 129
Self-reflection, 117
Self-respect, 53–69.
  See also Character
  and authenticity, 158
  building, 62–63
  and character, 58
  in children, 122
  and comparison, 64
  and conduct, 119
  definition of, 54
  and disrespect, 64
  erosion of, 62
  expression of, 53
  habits for, 7
  importance of, 8–9, 28
  internal nature of, 59
  and narcissism, 146
  and purpose, 110
  and reputation, 68
  from self-knowledge, 65
  and social media, 66–67
  teaching, 132
Sethi, Deepak, 51
Sheen Center for Thought and Culture, 4, 71–73, 80, 86, 136, 140, 158
Slouching Towards Bethlehem (Didion), 54
Small talk, 10, 44–49, 52, 131
Smith, Margaret Chase, 137–138
Smith, Phil, 10
Snark, 30
Snopes, 12
Social-emotional learning, 19, 129
Social interactions, 10, 14, 31, 71
Social isolation, 14, 30, 47, 153–154, 159. *See also* Loneliness
Social media:
  addiction to, 150
  anonymity of, 30, 64, 151–152
  and civility, 149
  comparison from, 66
  disagreement on, 29
  disrespectfulness of, 20–21
  effects on children, 13–15, 156
  encouragement from, 63
  engagement with, 63
  mistrust in, 12
  negative effects of, 19, 63
  and self-respect, 66–68
  viral nature of, 78
Standards, 15, 93, 102.
  See also Norms
Stanford Encyclopedia of Philosophy, 27, 54
Stanford University, 104

Index

Stefanik, Elise, 24–25
Sterne, Laurence, 43
Streep, Meryl, 12–13
Streisand, Barbra, 119
Sutton, Robert I., 104

T
Tap-out, 99–100
Target, 92
Taylor, James, 72
Tech-free zones, 14
Tecumseh, 37
Teixeira, José Micard, 12–13
Thompson, Hunter S., 8
Tibet House US, 40
TikTok, 22, 63, 150
To Kill a Mockingbird (novel), 156
Tolerance, 21, 78, 80, 137, 139, 144
Tolstoy, Leo, 19
Trujillo, Sol, 4, 10, 91–93, 105, 137, 151, 153
Trump, Donald J., 139
Trust building, 48, 59, 100
Tuncluer Textiles, 12
Twain, Mark, 94

U
UBS Investment Bank, 134
Unity, 83, 152, 155
University College Cork, 57
University of Connecticut, 34, 126
University of Houston, 99
University of Oregon, 109
University of Pittsburgh, 3, 108, 111
USA Today, 51

V
Values-in-Action Foundation, 4, 19–22, 128–139, 158

Vassar College, 23
VeryWell Mind magazine, 48
von Bidder, Alex, 3, 6, 39–44, 51, 59, 110, 121

W
Wake Up America Weekend (television program), 22–23
Waldinger, Robert, 120
Wall Street Journal, 23, 51, 90, 135
Washington, George, 41
Why a Cat Is Better Than a Man (Nolan), 50
Why Can't My Brother Be More Like My Cat? (Nolan), 84
Wiggins Learns His Manners at the Four Seasons Restaurant (von Bidder), 39, 122
Wilde, Oscar, 48
Wildish, Lee, 84
Williams, Bernie, 72
Williams, Venus, 69
Winfrey, Oprah, 114
Won't You Be My Neighbor? (film), 13, 33
Work Is Love Made Visible (Drucker), 93, 108, 112, 123
The Worrywart's Prayer Book (Nolan), 84

Y
Yale University, 90, 101
Yates, P. H., 152
Yoga, 51
Yousafzai, Malala, 5

Z
Zajechowski, Matt, 45
Zenger, Jack, 77